ASK

Questions That Create

A Principle That Works

It Is Given, Because You Asked

By

David Allen

(Creator of ASKffirmations)

It's not just asking questions. It's asking questions with the intention of creating experiences. It's how you ask that gives you the right feeling, which gives you the consciousness of already having your desire that makes your desire your reality.

September 2018

Legal

First Printing September 2018

ISBN: 978-0-9995435-5-9

*ASKffirmations is a term I coined in order to uniquely identify the technique that I have successfully applied in my own life and set it apart from other similar techniques. It isn't about asking better questions but rather to ask questions I already have the answers to, inserting them into the question, and asking "How did I do that?" which gives me the consciousness of already having my desire. What you possess in consciousness is given to you. Possess the fulfilled desire. There is inherent principle at work in the question that creates the experiences... the expression that the impression of the question makes. That is what ASKffirmations do.

A Metaphysical and the Law of Attraction Technique to Better Your Life by Giving You Better Experiences and Conditions Through Asking Defined Questions with Detailed Answers That YOU Choose.

The Subconscious Mind Does The Rest.

Contents

They're Affirmations, They're Questions, They're Creative, They're Magic.

You provide the Question and the Answer ... in the form of your fulfilled desire. Your Subconscious Mind gives you the experience. It's a Principle and it really is that simple.

Do not underestimate the power that this book which you hold in your hands has to transform your life the way you would like to transform it. There is a principle at work, and *that* is why it works.

Don't read this book in search of the secret. The secret is knowing the principle and *applying* the principle daily for the rest of your life. That's the secret.

"The man who at will can assume whatever state he pleases has found the keys to the Kingdom of Heaven." - *Neville Goddard*

"ASKffirmations are an assumption of the wish fulfilled, in question form." - *David Allen*

This book is dedicated to the loving memory of
Mariana Anderson Morse

Acknowledgements

A very special thank you to Gail Boynton for all her help on this book. It is very much appreciated and you have my deepest and sincerest gratitude.

My wife and daughter who have been a big support, inspiration and motivation for my being able to do what I love. I couldn't do what I do without you two.

To all the friends I have met online from CCOR to Facebook that have been a part of my journey in all that metaphysics has brought to my life, the compliments, the inspiration, the input and camaraderie that has been developed over the years, I appreciate you all more than you may ever know. I would not have grown as much as I have without you.

A group of like-minded people coming together for one purpose, to better all our lives. I think we have done just that and the journey will continue.

Your Greatest Discovery Will Be the Power and Magic of Your Own Thoughts ... Silent, Spoken or Written. ASKffirmations are one aspect of that.

David Allen

It is possible to resolve every situation by the proper use of Imagination. *Our task is to get the right sentence, the one which implies that our desire is realized, and fire the Imagination with it.* All this is intimately connected with the mystery of "the still small voice".

Neville Goddard

Our task is to get the right sentence, the one which implies that our desire is realized, and fire the Imagination with it.

THAT is what ASKffirmations do.

Foreword by Gail Boynton

What you are about to read has the potential of rocking your world *if* you are up to the task. I guarantee it will be well worth it.

When David Allen asked me to write the Foreword of his new book about questions, of course, it came in the form of a question. "How did I find someone to write the foreword to my upcoming book so easily?" Even though I recognized that as one of his carefully worded, magical questions - from the desire fulfilled - I still couldn't resist guessing who it might be.

After I offered a couple names, he finally said, "You! You were a part of it right from the beginning." He was kind enough not to mention that I had been hinting ... frequently ... in a not so subtle way ... that I *really* wanted him to write a book about the questions technique. I had found it to be a powerful method to affirm my desire in the form of a question already answered ... an answer already in existence. It felt very good, and I was seeing results all the time. Little did I know he had already started writing the book.

Let me start by saying that ASKffirmations are delightfully easy! There is nothing complicated about them. However, there *is* something required of *you* if you want to reap the rewards of a fantastic life. You need to pay attention to David's succinct instructions and see them through. An important take-away for me is that you must be willing to change your Thoughts to be in harmony with Universal Principles. If you start there, you will find that your specific desires will fall into place. And ASKffirmations are the tools that will turbo-charge your creative imagination and give your Subconscious Mind, your Genie, the clarity of your desires.

David provides the instruction and a wonderful list of examples to help you understand the structure of the most effective ASKffirmations. I read every single one of them, out loud, one right after the other. I highly recommend it because it felt awesome. I felt a stirring within ... a progression upward in consciousness ... as I read them.

After you have read this amazing book, you will own a vital piece of understanding to your spiritual journey, and you will be inspired to create your own custom, life-changing ASKffirmations.

THERE'S YOUR POWER!

How did you know that ASKffirmations were *your* key to a magical life?

Introduction

This is a book about questions, words, Metaphysics, mind, the Law of Attraction and all things related to creation and being a creator.

While the main point is to reveal how our questions are creative of our experiences, it is just as important to show how various other factors of mind come into play. The more we know about anything, the better our skill will be.

The book you hold in your hand is the result of over ten years of self-examination, reading hundreds of metaphysical books from the last 100 or so years from some of the best authors on how creation and attraction work, hundreds of hours meditating and sitting in the silence, hundreds of conversations with others who have the exact same interests, recognizing the impact in my own life and seeing the effect it has had in the lives of others who have applied the very same principles in their own lives.

It is a book showing one powerful technique by which we can create our reality without effort while making it fun and easy, as well. The right questions give us the consciousness of already having our desires, and that is how attraction works.

Without application of the principle, which this book outlines, this book will do very little for you. Until it is converted into your own experience, through application, it is nothing more than theory. Give it a chance, and you will be amazed at how it transforms your life for the better.

Information is contained in the book, however the wisdom comes from knowing what to apply, how to apply it, why we should apply it and ultimately applying it.

Very important note: This book does not have the power to do for you what only you can do for yourself. All it can do is show you the principle and how and why it works, but if you do not understand and apply the principle, you will never see the desired results in your own life. All too often I have seen people say that something simply doesn't work, or list reasons why it doesn't work, when their own words were a confession that they either didn't understand or didn't work with the principle. They seemed to rely on their logic or past experiences as the only determining factors as to whether a principle worked or was true. This is *not* how you conclude the truth of any metaphysical teaching. Without putting principles to the test, yourself, you are not likely to realize the truth that so many are seeking ... the truth that has set so many free from the conditions in their lives.

You cannot test metaphysical principles one time, a day, a week, a month or year. To do so is to miss the point of these teachings altogether. This is about changing the way you think for the remainder of your life by making certain principles the foundation of your thinking.

While I could go on, I do not think it would prove anything to a doubter, and the ones who know these truths do not need a lengthier explanation. I merely mention it here for those who may be a little unsure about how principles work and would benefit by knowing that the *key* is to apply the teachings as opposed to merely reading them then asking others for their opinions about whether the teachings are true and whether they work.

You must either prove the principles to yourself, or forever be lacking the desired results that so many others have gained from understanding the laws and principles and applying them in their own lives.

David Allen

Authors Preface

I have made it my life's ambition to understand Metaphysics and The Law of Attraction for more than a decade. I knew they contained secrets, information, and knowledge of which most people are not aware. From day one of my initial discovery of metaphysical teachings I lived and breathed everything I could find on the subject. I didn't just want to know *how* ... I wanted to know *why,* and I wanted to experience what these teachings promised.

When you think about anything for any extended period, answers will come to you. I found out, not just by reading, but by implementing in my life what I learned. I put teachings to the test myself. I wanted more than knowledge. I wanted the actual experiences that comes out of that knowledge.

Most people will know that something works but will not be entirely sure why. If we don't know why something works, we may not be able to understand it well enough to make it work to our advantage on a consistent basis. Metaphysics *does* have all the answers we need regarding how our minds work. You will be greatly rewarded for investing your time into the study of Metaphysics.

Everything in life can be improved ... everything. Look around you - cars, phones, planes, cameras, homes, home appliances, clothing and computers. All these things continue to make our lives better every day, and there is always someone finding a way to improve on them. We can apply the same idea in our lives by finding new ways to create.

This is what ASKffirmations are. An improvement on bettering our lives, bettering the lives of those who understand the principle behind it, and applying it.

ASKffirmations are not tangible. You cannot hold them in your hand like you would a physical object. It is up to the user of this principle to see, feel, and experience the difference it will make in one's life ... to know that one possesses a pearl of a great price.

Those who know what principles are know that it is in the application of the principle that the results are secured in one's life. You must make it a part of you, who you are, what you believe, until it *becomes* who you are. Do not look for results in a day or a month or a year. The desired results will come. This is true of any principle which we apply to our lives.

This principle is *not* just to be used to manifest things. It is intended to better your life on all levels, all phases, and in doing so all those things you previously desired will start to appear in your life. When that happens, observe. You will *know* that the magic your life is now revealing has occurred *because* of something so simple that you will wonder why you never knew it before.

What is it that made life a joy for you? What is it that made you feel good all the time? What is it that made you see life in a completely different way than you ever imagined you could?

A Principle.

It is said that we are creators. This is a truth.

However, if you are not awake to this truth, you are *not* consciously creating your life in the way you would if you were awake to consciously making the choices because of your new-found awareness on *how* we are creators.

It is my hope and desire that you become imaginatively awake to the wonders of the human mind ... of its capability ... of how our beliefs shape our lives ... of how those things we say that we know shape our lives ... how those things to which we agree shape our lives.

It is my hope you understand that you must know certain things about certain aspects of our being to honestly say you are awake and consciously creating your life, to know that if you don't know how suggestions from outer sources, for example, can shape our lives, those outer suggestions, can do just that.

Be aware of what you give your attention to. Be aware of your own Thoughts, your own beliefs about what it means to think OF something rather than think FROM the wish fulfilled.

These are some of the things that shape our lives. Some of the most important things.

When you start applying ASKffirmations daily in your life, you *will* feel different, you *will* feel better. That is the only sign you need to *know* that ASKffirmations are working to better your life. Trust this process.

However, if you think you can ask these questions, and money, health and love become yours forever then go back to your old ways, not only will those manifestations no longer continue to occur, but when you give up living this principle you will have given up on what the principle will do for you. You will lose what you have.

To those who have this understanding, much is given, to those who don't, that which they do have will be taken from them.

The principle is a way of life. It is not reciting a few affirmations once or twice a day and expecting miracles. In order to profit from principles, we must understand them and apply them.

Once you understand this, there is one more action you should take. Be grateful and appreciative that you *now* know one of the greatest secrets known to the world ... that you are now in possession of something so great, so wonderful, so amazing that you will wonder how you never knew it before.

You can create your life. You can make all your dreams come true, because now you know the very things that shape and mold the reality around you and that you are creating it.

Make ASKffirmations a daily practice.

In this book I present the following ASKffirmations as a sample. Only you know what you desire. Get creative. Write your ASKffirmations down. Look at them often. Say them often.

Keep your most sacred ASKffirmations to yourself. We do not say them with the intention to just have fun, although they are fun, but to create our reality, to better our lives, to see for ourselves that what we are always telling ourselves, those questions we ask, those things we are always feeling, giving our attention to and agreeing with, IS our reality and that when we change what we tell ourselves our outer reality matches it. The world is our mirror.

The point of the book is to provide you with the principle, not to prove to anyone what works and what doesn't. As anyone who has studied metaphysics should know, principles are not something one proves to another but must be individually put to the test and proven to oneself.

David Allen

Chapter One

I AM YOUR Subconscious Mind

Hi... I AM YOUR SUBCONSCIOUS MIND.

Do you hear me? The words you are reading RIGHT NOW are coming from me, YOUR Subconscious Mind.

I AM speaking to YOU, the reader.

I know you want things to change in your life. I know you want better and improved conditions.

So why do you keep telling people why you feel so bad?

Why do you tell people how hard things are for you?

Why are you giving your attention to things that make you feel bad? Why are you telling people these things?

How do you expect conditions in your life to improve when you are always saying the wrong things?

Why are you reacting to negative people?

Why don't you just stop all that? When you do I will stop giving you things of a negative nature.

Don't you know that it is YOUR words that are creating your feelings, and your feelings are creating your conditions and experiences?

Don't you know that you are telling people how you feel INSTEAD of telling yourself how YOU desire to feel?

You see, I AM listening to you too. When you tell others, you are also telling me. When you tell me, I will always make you feel the way you SAY you feel.

You are not helping your cause by always telling people that you feel bad. You are not helping your cause by telling people how hard it is to speak good things. You're not helping your cause by giving your ATTENTION to negative Thoughts and things.

I AM ALWAYS listening to you. Yes, ME, YOUR SUBCONSCOUS MIND. I AM ALWAYS LISTENING, and I AM ALWAYS giving you what you ASK for.

Don't you KNOW that your words are creating how you feel? Do you really not know this?

Don't you KNOW that you can't tell me, your Subconscious Mind, that you don't feel good? Your words are my instructions. Tell me you feel good, and I will make you feel good.

Every single time you tell me, your Subconscious Mind, that you do not feel good I WILL GRANT YOUR WISH, and you will NOT FEEL GOOD. I can only do what you ask me to do.

I AM YOUR Subconscious Mind. I, YOUR Subconscious Mind, GRANT your EVERY WISH, your EVERY DESIRE.

Do not EVER tell me, "I Feel Bad" because I WILL make you feel bad.

Don't EVER tell me, "Life Is Hard" because I WILL make life hard for you, but only because you asked.

I told you ... I GRANT ... YOUR ... EVERY ... WISH.

I AM the Genie of YOUR life. I AM YOUR Subconscious Mind.

When YOU say... "I"... When you say the WORD, "I," that is MY CUE to do as YOU wish. "I Feel..." "I AM..." "I Have..." "I Can..." these are your wishes, and I, your Subconscious Mind will grant them, every time.

"I Feel Good" is your wish, and it is MY command ... Your Subconscious Mind ... MY Command to MAKE you feel good.

But as long as you don't say it, I can't just do it for you. You will have to ask. You must tell me what you desire to feel, and I will grant you your wish.

The reason you feel any less than good is because you are thinking bad Thoughts. You are giving your attention to bad things, or you are talking to others, telling them how bad you feel. But guess what? I, your Subconscious Mind, am ALSO listening to you, and when you tell others you feel bad, I hear you as well, and I WILL make you feel bad, because that is YOUR ORDER to ME, your Subconscious Mind, to make you feel bad. I Grant Your Every Wish and Desire.

And do you know what your every wish and desires is?

It is your WORDS that you speak ... it's not what you WANT ... it is what YOU are SPEAKING, what you are THINKING, what you put in WRITING.

"I Feel Good" is a DESIRE. It is a WISH.

If you want ME, your Subconscious Mind, to make you feel good, then you will have to SAY to yourself, "I FEEL GOOD."

So, let me, your Subconscious Mind, help you.

SPEAK what you want to feel, not HOW you feel, but how you DESIRE to feel. "I FEEL GOOD." Isn't THAT your desire? Then say it and say it often.

If you feel bad, then SAY, "I FEEL GOOD" and I WILL make you feel good.

If you're feeling down, SAY, "I FEEL GOOD." Say it often every single day, and I WILL make you feel good.

I AM YOUR Subconscious Mind ... and I can make you feel anyway you want me to make you feel.

However, YOU have to know HOW to say it.

You DO NOT say, "I WANT to feel good."

Do you know why?

Because when you say, "I want to feel good," what you are telling me is you do not already feel good. Wanting, wishing, needing is implying that you do not already have what it is you desire to have.

I grant EVERY WISH.

It's not what you WANT or NEED or WISH.

It's what you SAY and FEEL. Claim it.

"I Feel Good" IS your command to me, your Subconscious Mind, to make you feel good.

If you say, "I Feel Bad," that is ALSO YOUR command to ME, your Subconscious Mind, to make YOU feel bad.

You MUST learn my language. I AM your Subconscious Mind, and you MUST learn MY Language.

I do not respond to wishes and needs and wants in the way you think I do.

I, your Subconscious Mind, respond to what you SAY you ARE... NOT what you want, wish or need.

When YOU... the one reading this right now... say "I," that is MY cue, your Subconscious Mind, MY cue to grant your wish. Whatever YOU say after "I" is added unto you, and it is I, your Subconscious Mind, that will do it. "I AM," not "I Will."

Do you NOW see MY, your Subconscious Mind's, POWER?

What YOU add to "I" or "I AM" is YOUR command to ME, your Subconscious Mind. When you say, "I," YOUR Subconscious Mind is listening, awaiting your cue. You are literally summoning ME, your Subconscious Mind, to do YOUR Bidding. You are INVOKING me. Go ahead ... look up the word, "INVOKE" in the dictionary, so you know what it means that YOU are INVOKING ME, your Subconscious Mind, to grant YOUR wish.

I ... The WORD, I, is MY, YOUR Subconscious Mind's, COMMAND to do as YOU wish.

I, Your Subconscious Mind, AM the Genie of YOUR life. I, YOUR Subconscious Mind, can do ANYTHING you desire, but you must know how to ASK me, YOUR Subconscious Mind, using the WORD, I. Otherwise I can't do it for you.

Do you see? Do you understand? Do you KNOW that every time you say the WORD "I" it is your command to ME, your Subconscious Mind, to do what YOU ASK?

"I" is ASKING.

You do not say, "I want this or that."

You do not say, "I need this or that."

Do you know why you do not say, "I want?"

Do you know why you do not say, "I wish?"

Do you know why you do not say, "I need?"

Because that is telling me, YOUR Subconscious Mind, that you DO NOT ALREADY possess the feeling of having your desire or wish or need or want, and I, therefore, cannot give you what you really desire. You must understand the language. What you possess in consciousness is what I, your Subconscious Mind, will give you as an experience.

For me, YOUR Subconscious Mind, to give YOU your desires, you must add your desire to the WORD, "I" ... "feel good," ... "love life," etc. These are the things you add to "I".

"I HAVE an Abundance of Health" is HOW you ask me, YOUR Subconscious Mind, for your desire of Health.

When you say, "I want Health" what you are telling me, your Subconscious Mind, is that you do not already have it in consciousness, so that is what I, your Subconscious Mind, will give you... which would be NO HEALTH.

Do you see how I, your Subconscious Mind, takes instructions?

You should not ask me like you would ask another person.

You CLAIM it in Consciousness FIRST.

"I AM" and "I HAVE" are TWO commands to me that will allow me, your Subconscious Mind, to fulfill your desire.

That is HOW you must ASK me.

Not by saying, "Can I have," but by saying "I HAVE."

Let me, your Subconscious Mind, give you more insight into HOW I work.

When YOU say, "I Have," this first goes into your consciousness, and from there, I, your Subconscious Mind, pick up THAT vibration, that feeling and make it an external reality for you.

Just how I, your Subconscious Mind, do that is MY Secret.

No one knows how I, your Subconscious Mind, turns your Thoughts into things in your life. My ways are past finding out. All you can know of me, your Subconscious Mind, is HOW I work, not HOW I do what I do. That is MY secret.

What is it you desire?

A car?

How would you ask me, your Subconscious Mind, for this car that you desire?

Would you say, "I want a car"? "I really need this car"? "I would really like this car"? "I wish I had this car"?

Or, would you command me, your Subconscious Mind, to give you your desire by getting the consciousness of ALREADY having it?

Can you use your imagination?

Can you visualize?

Can you see yourself driving the car you desire?

Can you feel your hands wrapped around the steering wheel?

Can you see yourself driving this car down the road?

Can you feel the seats?

Can you see this car in your driveway?

Can you hear your friends telling you what a beautiful car you now have?

Can you see your friends sitting in the passenger seat?

When you think these things, I know what you desire. Because when you think these things, you are giving me the blueprint for just what it is you desire.

Get to know me, your Subconscious Mind. Just learn how to speak to me so that I know what to give you, and I WILL give it to you.

I AM the Genie of Your Life! You Have Unlimited 'Wishes'.

Your 'Wish' Is My Command!

Chapter Two

What Are ASKffirmations?

In short, ASKffirmations are questions that you ask yourself, which elicit the experience because the answer you choose to give is in your question. The question and the answer, both provided by you, give you the consciousness of already having your desire, which is the cause of the experience becoming your reality.

ASKffirmations create the experience (draw the actual experience to you via The Law of Attraction) by giving you the consciousness of the fulfilled desire, because the fulfilled desire is in the form of the answer being *in* the question.

ASKffirmations never ask ..."Why *do* I." They ask in past tense ... "How *did* I." The difference between these 2 methods is that one way is seeking answers assuming you don't already know the answer, which is thinking OF and not FROM the fulfilled desire; and the other is already in possession of the answer (which is the actual thing to be brought into expression) in consciousness and is using this understanding to make the expression happen in reality.

ASKffirmations are creative and designed to give you the experience, not just an answer in words, unless that is what you seek. The experience is what you desire, and you get it by applying the principle of providing the answer in the question.

It's Your Question, Your Answer, Your Experience!

There is no one to turn to but self.

A TRUE ASKffirmation never asks WHY.

Do you know why? Because you put *your* answer *in* the question. When you ask *how*, past tense, which is thinking FROM the end, you are eliciting the experience, not seeking an answer. Asking, "How did I" is giving you the consciousness of already possessing your fulfilled desire.

All questions are good, as they will bring you answers, but ASKffirmations will bring you the *experience* you choose. What you hold in consciousness is the reality you are creating.

Asking, "Why?" does give me answers, but asking "How did I" is designed to give me experiences.

An ASKffirmation is an affirmation (your desire, your answer) put into question form, which elicits the experience. The definition of elicit that I use here is: **To draw forth (something that is latent or potential) into existence.** By giving *our* answer, the answer we choose to *our* question, and knowing that *how* to ask is very important, we are literally drawing forth our latent desires, into existence... and this is done by possessing the desire already in consciousness. When consciousness has the answer, the Subconscious gives us the expression, and that is how we create the experience ... our realty. Make the right impression, and you get the right expression.

ASKffirmations aren't *just* about asking better questions. They are about being as specific as you can to manifest the reality of your choosing and then phrasing your question (how you ask is what you are seeking here) so it is understood that it is already done. (Refer to Neville Goddard's teaching of Imagining FROM the END and not OF the end.) This creates the consciousness of having, the feeling of already having. Your question must have the fulfilled desire (the answer) IN the question and that is the creative act. This gives you the *feeling* that it is done and attracts the experience to you. We are always creating by our Thoughts, but when we create in this manner

(ASKffirmations) the experience will be as a result of your question (how you ask) and your answer (the wish fulfilled). You *are* your *own* Genie. Your Subconscious *is* your Genie. You are one with your Subconscious. Your Thoughts become the things in your life ... the experiences in your life.

You are *not* seeking an answer by asking a question. You *are* asking for the sole purpose of creating the experience by putting your own answer *in* the question. If it is an answer you seek, you would ask the question, "How did I get that answer so easily?" and this will bring the answer to you.

The secret of an ASKffirmation is *how* you ask and *how* you answer ... not after you ask the question... but by inserting the answer *in* the question. This creates the state-of-mind, where creation occurs, in consciousness, and why the experience is drawn to you. When you have the consciousness of already possessing your desire, which is the reason for asking and answering (this creates the feeling of possession), you are literally drawing your desire into your life as an actual experience.

You are actually eliciting (drawing forth your desire that is latent or potential, into existence), the experience with an ASKffirmation.

The world in which we live is truly a mirror of what we possess in consciousness.

In order to have, you must be.

In order to have your desire you must be in possession of it in consciousness first.

The *Law* is very clear. That which we possess in consciousness and hold in consciousness will be our outer expression in life. We must make the right impression in order to get the right expression.

26

The differences between *how* and *why* are very subtle. To one who is not aware of how consciousness works they would not be able to spot the difference, the most important difference. They would think they would both accomplish the same thing, but they would be wrong.

They both are questions that are seeking something. One is seeking possession of an answer, of which it could then possess in consciousness and subsequently have the experience drawn to them. However, as long as the question remains as wanting to know why, the experience can't be drawn to them. The Subconscious simply does not have the right information to do what you would like it to do. When you know that mind is creative, you can eliminate the need to ask why, and instead, give the Subconscious the fulfilled desire, so that it may bring it into expression.

The other already has possession of the answer, which seeks to get the expression by presenting the right question to the Subconscious. By knowing the answer already and stating that we would like to know *how*, we have given our Subconscious the means by which it can make our desire our reality.

A change in consciousness (impression) is a change in expression.

The right ASKffirmations creates the right state-of-mind. The right state-of-mind creates the right expression.

ASKffirmations

ASKffirmation: The creative action of wording a question to elicit a reality of your choosing. (This is one definition).

Affirmation: The action or process of affirming something.

Question: A sentence worded or expressed so as to elicit information. (In the case of an ASKffirmation where the answer is in the question, what we are eliciting, is the experience)

Elicit: Draw forth (something that is latent or potential) into existence.

Assumption: A thing that is accepted as true or as certain to happen, without proof.

Imagination: The ability of the mind to be creative or resourceful.

Be sure to visit **nevillegoddardbooks.com**. We have thousands of free metaphysical and law of attraction books that you can either read online or download in PDF for free. All Neville Goddard books can be read there for free as well. Many of these books are the very books that allowed me to discover this technique.

ASKffirmations are creative statements that you put into question form which elicits your reality through the process of Assumption. Do not focus on the absence of your desire in the outer world. You are creating it in consciousness first, then allowing the Subconscious to bring it into expression.

Think FROM the End, Not OF the End - Neville Goddard

Imagination Creates Reality - Neville Goddard

Assumptions Harden Into Fact - Neville Goddard

Consciousness Is the Only Reality - Neville Goddard

You are literally drawing into existence a reality that you choose by the way (how) you ask the question.

It's a Question. It's an Affirmation. It has the answer in it. It's Creative. It's Your Reality. It brings the experience to you.

This technique allows you to turn any affirmation into a question, which allows you to draw forth into existence a reality that you have chosen with your ASKffirmation.

How you word the question is how you choose your reality.

Affirmation: I AM One with the Very Power That Created Me

ASKffirmation: How did I become one with the very power that created me?

"How *did* I?" is what brings the experience into your reality because it creates the feeling in consciousness that the works are done. It has assumed that you are already one with the power that created you. Therefore, you do not have to seek this power. Your question already did that.

The affirmation can also do that. So why the need for the ASKffirmation? Many have said that affirmations seem like a lie to them. By simply turning the affirmation into a question of how you did it, your conscious mind no longer feels like it is a lie, and it puts you in a different state-of-mind.

A true ASKffirmation requires *nothing* more than to ask the question. That is the planting of the seed. How it comes to you is not your concern. Your job is to simply ask and trust that your seed (the questions) will be your harvest (your experiences).

There is really nothing more to do than get the consciousness of already having your desire and then allowing it to unfold in your life. Your actions do not create your reality, your Thoughts do ... silent, spoken or written ... and asking questions FROM the wish fulfilled is a tried and tested method that works for those who understand the entire principle.

There are similar questions that leave you wanting an answer to your question. ASKffirmations take away that feeling of wanting by answering your own question and allowing you to have the experience within, which creates the experience without.

"Life Is *so* good." (This is an Affirmation).

"Why is life so good?" (This is *not* an ASKffirmation. It leaves you wanting to know why life is so good, *and* it says nothing about life being good for *you*. That is non-specific.)

"How did I create a life that is so good by asking this question?" (This IS an ASKffirmation. It contains the question with the answer, which gives you the experience within, which will be the experience without).

At first glance you may think you are simply asking how and seeking an answer but look closer. It assumes that your life is already *so* good, and it did so by asking this question. Now all that's left is for the Subconscious to bring the experience into expression.

If your actions help you have better Thoughts, use those actions as a helpmate. However, just realize that it is still your Thoughts (silent, spoken or written) that are doing the creating, *not* your actions. Do not put emphasis on action being the creator. This will lead you astray from where your concentration needs to be focused ... on Thought ... either silent, spoken or written. Thought has many forms, these are 3 of them. The 3 big ones.

If your mind is on action, or if you want to know more about action, there are schools and teachings that teach that. Metaphysics teaches the power of mind, consciousness, Thought.

ASKffirmations are a metaphysical and Law of Attraction technique. Questions that one asks themselves where the answer, the wish fulfilled, is in the question and put there by the questioner. The question is merely asked with the desire already fulfilled, which is the actual creative act. All that is left is for your Subconscious Mind to give the experience that you created in your mind.

Those who have the feeling of already having their desire are obeying a law of mind, of being, which is how things are drawn to us. It is how the Law of Attraction works. If you desire to attract something, you create a state-of-mind where your wish is already fulfilled, and "It will be done unto you." Feeling is the secret. The works are done.

Your questions should create the feeling of already having (in consciousness) your desire.

When you understand this technique, you will no longer ask *how*-to do something, since how to do it is simply to *ask* the right question. That is the creative act. To ask how you *did* it.

This is asking questions FROM the wish fulfilled. (Neville Goddard is a great source for understanding why we think FROM and not OF the wish fulfilled. His teachings will give more understanding of why ASKffirmations work so well).

You will then be provided with reasons why you already feel good (experiences) rather than how to go about doing it. You will, therefore, be eliminating the need to figure out how to do it and allowing the laws of being, the laws of mind, the power of Thought, of words, to do the rest for you.

The question is intended to provide you with experiences and conditions that you provided by asking the question, as well as the providing the answer you choose.

That's it in a nutshell.

You are choosing *your* reality.

"It is always possible to pass from thinking OF the end you desire to realize, to thinking FROM the end. But the crucial matter is thinking FROM the end, for thinking FROM means unification or fusion with the idea: whereas in thinking OF the end, there is always subject and object – the thinking individual and the thing Thought. You must imagine yourself into the state of your wish fulfilled, in your love for that state, and in so doing, live and think from it and no more of it. You pass from thinking of, to thinking from, by centering your imagination in the feeling of the wish fulfilled." - Neville Goddard

It is very important to stress the teachings of Neville Goddard as it will give insight into why ASKffirmations are so effective. Thinking FROM the END ... asking the question FROM the END. The works are done. You *ask*, and it is given. You ask the question and are given the experience as the answer. Without knowing the importance of thinking FROM the wish fulfilled, you might begin to question this technique, which may affect your results.

Consciousness is the *only* reality. Assumptions harden into fact. Imagination creates reality. Feeling is the secret.   All are Neville Goddard teachings.

Our Thought is literally creating our lives. To know this is to know the truth. Words are Thoughts. We can enter any state-of-mind at any time we choose, and the ASKffirmation technique is one of many ways to do that.

Everyone has a preferred method of doing things. ASKffirmations are one more option for those who feel that they have not found the one that works best for them. Many have already proven to their own satisfaction that ASKffirmations do, indeed, give them the results they seek.

If this technique does not work for you, it means that you might benefit from a different method. Find what works best for you. Use that one. There is no way that you can know for sure whether any teachings will give you the desired results until you test them for yourself. Otherwise, they are simply theories.

ASKffirmations are intended to draw forth into existence a reality of your choosing. Those answers can come in many forms. Maybe it will be money that comes into your life. Maybe it will be Health or Love, or your dream job, or a long-awaited vacation that the means of which were brought to you *because* you *asked.*

The Subconscious Mind *always* answers our questions, even though we have given the answer in words, the Subconscious Mind answers with experiences and circumstances. It doesn't ask you, "Are you sure?" It answers because you asked and it's up to *you* to know *how* to ask to get the experience of your choice.

The more specific your questions are, the more specific your answers are, the more specific your experiences will be.

Powerful, right? You bet it is.

Once you start applying these questions to yourself 24/7/365, your life *will* begin to change into what *you* want it to be. It is your creation. You will see that there is no one to turn to but self to create your own reality.

From the time we began thinking for ourselves, we have been creating our own reality. When we are asleep to the truth that our Thoughts (including questions) are creating our reality, we create unwanted conditions that we never would have created had we known what we were saying to ourselves.

The following holds THE KEY to successful ASKfirmations. Read it repeatedly until you fully grasp it.

When you are considering YOUR question...it is during this phase of asking that YOU provide the answer WITHIN the question. It is your answer that will be given to you as your experience.

Do you want to feel good all the time?

Of course, you do. Who wouldn't?

So how would you ask for this so that it is given unto you as *you* ask?

Would you ask, "Why do I feel good?"

Or would you ask, "How did I discover the secret to always feeling good all the time was to say, I Feel Good?"

That's it. Be specific.

There are no limitations in that question.

It is assuming you already feel good all the time.

You answer is already built into the question.

The signs that follow will be *you* feeling good *all* the time. That is the experience that will be given to you.

You are not to do this for an hour a day. This is how you should think from now on. All day, every day.

Be careful, though. If you expect results to happen immediately and start looking for signs instead of allowing them to come to you, you will be breaking *one* of the cardinal rules of ASKffirmations. Once you have established the state-of-mind where you are thinking FROM the end, where your wish is already fulfilled, then things will happen. Your reality will match your state-of-mind. Why would you look for signs when you know mind is creative, and you already created it in your mind with your Thoughts. Let the world be the mirror of your consciousness.

You will not look for results... You will *observe* them.

See the difference?

When the experiences present themselves, acknowledge them. Be grateful for them, appreciate them. Literally, say to yourself, "Thank You!" That, as well, will make you feel good. Over a very short time, if you *live* by this principle and really understand the technique, your life will reflect *all* your desires all the time.

Now, do not go back to your old ways. Don't watch negative things or read negative things or talk with people who want to talk about negative things.

When you fully grasp this technique and apply it, you will see that it is you who asks, you who answers and you who are responsible for the experience.

Start living your new life!

Affirm your new life, create your new life. Do it with ASKffirmations.

ASKffirmations

It's *how* you ask the question that
determines your experience.

When you ask the right question, a specific question,
and put a specific answer in the question,
you'll get your specific desire.

The Answer is *in* the Question. Because *you* put it there.

Make the question and answer give you
the experience you choose!

ASK and It Is Given unto You!

The only action that is required by you is to *ask* the
question. The Subconscious Mind does the rest.

ASKffirmations are always asked in past tense,
never in present tense.

These are not *just* questions. These questions are, literally,
creative of the conditions in our lives.

NEVER ask a question about a negative. Meaning ... do not
ask why something is or why you feel a certain way, if in fact
you do not want to feel the way about which the question is
asking. Just know that you do feel something that you don't
want to feel and start applying what you know. "I feel good,"
or "How did I end up always feeling good?"

How we word questions, or anything for that matter, has
everything to do with the experiences we receive.

Do not take this lightly. Your questions are creative of
conditions. They are not *just* to get answers in words, but to
get actual experiences.

Chapter Three

What ASKffirmations Are and What They Are NOT.

The intention behind an ASKffirmation is *not* to make you feel better. The purpose is to create a better reality for you in which to exist by having and holding these questions in your consciousness. As they drop into your Subconscious Mind, the answers/experiences will surface when *you* are ready to hear them, when you are ready to accept them, when you are ready to experience them.

Consciousness Is the Only Reality - Neville Goddard

When we fill our minds with these questions, we are filling our consciousness with our fulfilled desires. By continuing to create the state-of-mind of fulfilled desires, the Subconscious Mind takes you at your word. It then seeks to bring into expression what *you* have accepted as your truth. Don't concern yourself with the means of bringing your desire into expression. That is the job of the Subconscious, its ways (The Subconscious Mind) are past finding out. You are merely giving it the instructions (the fulfilled desire) and by deduction, it will bring the experience to you. Those who are asleep to how this works will wonder how you accomplish what you do, but you know the secret. Life has always worked this way but being aware that it works this way makes you a conscious creator of your own reality.

If you would like more insight on how the Subconscious Mind works, my book, 'The Secrets, Mysteries and Powers of The Subconscious Mind' is available at Amazon.com and other online bookstores.

Chapter Four

Instructions for Getting Results

To get results from ASKffirmations they *must* become *your* questions, *your* answers (the answers being IN the question.) They do not work if you think of them as someone else's questions. You must validate them, confirm them to be true of you. This does not mean that you must make all ASKffirmations yours. What you must do is choose which ones are yours, whether they were formed by someone else or you. Once they become yours, you have set in motion the principle that makes it your reality. You will then have the consciousness of having your fulfilled desire, which is what makes it your outer reality.

You would not say these one or two times and expect them to do what they are intended to do any more than you would say an affirmation once or twice. Say them often. Pick one or two to get started. Once you get the results and master one or two, you will then know that they work. Then you can expand and recreate your entire life using ASKffirmations.

Have fun with ASKffirmations. Have fun with your new reality. Enjoy life like you have never enjoyed it before.

Make this your new way of creating the reality of your choosing.

It works.

As with *any* metaphysical teaching, if you do not believe it will work, it will not work. So, if it does not seem to be working, you may want to consider that you really do not believe that they work. The fault does not lie in the principle but the operator of that principle.

This is the most profound technique that I've learned since delving into metaphysics. Life changing!!! - Kimberleigh Hogan-Lee

It's not just asking. It's HOW you ask!! - Lynette Williams

These questions are intended to change your mindset, to put you in a state-of-mind *where you possess your desire in consciousness, and the condition is brought to life out of the nothingness because you asked. Examine these and then create your own, and watch your life become magical by way of ASKffirmations.*

Chapter Five

The Questions

How did I discover the true hidden meanings of words that have eluded mankind for ages allowing all my desires to be fulfilled so easily?

How did I discover ALL the highest meanings of all the greatest teachings that have ever been given to mankind which allowed me to do things I have only ever wondered and dreamed about previously?

How did I learn how to think in such a way that life is no longer a mystery for me?

How did I make every single moment of my life a joy to live by simply thinking of the word, joy, every day?

How did my life become a constant flow of miracles and blessings by acknowledging that it was already so?

How did I discover true happiness, which I was searching for all my life, was as easy as saying, "I AM happy," and saying it often?

How did I always attract amazing, wonderful, caring, compassionate, powerful, beautiful, giving, genuine, wise, open, receptive, brilliant, strong, joyous, courageous, inspiring people into my life by believing that is all that existed?

The Answer Is Always in The Question Because We Put It There. The Experience Is Always the Result of That Question and Answer. We Always Choose Our Own Reality by Having the Consciousness of Our Fulfilled Desire.

How did the love I always feel for myself cause me to succeed at everything in life?

How did I find all the keys to a happy, successful, rewarding, satisfying life by focusing on these words?

How did I awaken to a life as an amazing creator by thinking about being an amazing creator?

How did I discover which Thoughts would give me the most amazing experiences I could have ever imagined?

How did my questions wake me up to a realization of health, prosperity and love that I Thought was only possible to others?

How did I make all my dreams a reality by asking how did I make all my dreams a reality?

How did I discover that my own personal questions were the best method known to man for bringing any desire I chose to fruition?

How did I discover that my questions were the answers I was seeking to getting my experiences?

How did I realize that my questions are the best way to create feelings that cause my desires to manifest in such a rapid manner?

How did I discover that by helping others achieve all their dreams that I was, in fact, also achieving all my dreams?

How did this question open the channels for love to flow
so freely into my life all the time?

How did I create such an overflowing abundance of love
in my life by asking this question?

How did I create such an ever-increasing and never-
ending abundance of wealth by way of my own
questions?

**The Secret of Deliberate Creation
Is Knowing How to Ask.**

How did my health improve so rapidly by asking, "How
did my health improve so rapidly"?

How did I realize that my answers to my questions
made my dreams come true faster than any other
method?

How did I discover that by asking how I attracted all the
best people into my life I was causing all the best people
to come into my life?

How did I always attract the most loving, caring, compassionate, kind people to surround me and impact my life in such amazing and powerful ways?

How did I realize the power I possess to ask any question I want, and have it manifest as the conditions and experiences in my life?

How did I discover the secret of how and why life only gave me the best experiences I asked for?

How did I realize that my questions were creating my reality which made me ask better questions to create a better reality?

How did I learn the secret to ask amazing questions and then have the answers I chose always show up immediately as my experiences?

How did I realize that the only action I ever have to take to change my reality is to ask the right questions and give my own answers?

How did I know that "I AM" is infinitely more powerful in creating my reality than "I Will" or "I Can"?

How did I eliminate the need to take action to change my life, and instead, turn to Thoughts to change it, and all action after that was with my new reality?

How did I know that my questions were creating my reality faster than any other thing I have ever done?

How did I figure out that I can create *any* reality I choose by asking the right questions with my specific answers?

How did I know that my reality is created within and experienced without by doing nothing more than asking questions?

The Answer Is Always in The Question, The Experience Is Always the Result of The Question and Answer.

How did I create such an amazing reality by asking the right questions and giving the most amazing answers?

How did I realize my Thoughts (silent, spoken or written) were the only thing I needed to create any reality I desired?

How did I improve my memory so easily by thanking my Subconscious Mind for always improving my memory so quickly?

How did I realize that by putting into my question the answer that I desired to experience, I would manifest that desire instantly?

How did I discover all the various ways to create a more abundant reality by asking for all the various ways to create a more abundant reality to be revealed to me?

How did my asking questions show me that everything in life was so much easier after I asked the right questions?

How did I realize I could pull important and valuable Thoughts out of the ethers so easily and successfully whereby I was able to transform my life and that of others by asking how I did it?

How did my asking questions reveal to me all that life has to offer in the shortest amount of time possible?

How did I learn a new word that made understanding the law of attraction so much clearer?

How did I not only realize that all things are possible, but that I could do anything using the powers that are latent within my mind by knowing I had already done it?

How did I realize that the appreciation I have of anything was the very key to drawing more abundance of anything into my life and not just the thing for which I had appreciation?

How did I realize that that my questions were the very thing that transformed my life from one of lack to one of abundance and prosperity?

My Answers to My Questions Are Always Creating My Reality.

How did I realize that the experiences I desired out of life were entirely dependent on me asking the right questions and giving the answer that would create those experiences?

How did I attract all the right books into my life so that I always had all answers to anything I desired to know at my fingertips?

How did I know all the right questions to ask for all the things I desired to experience in life?

How did I discover the most amazing questions that created the most amazing feelings so that my life became so magical that I never once doubted the power of my own questions again?

How did I discover that as I removed all the negatives from my Thoughts, it removed all the negatives from my life, and my life was positive and abundant in all things good from that moment on?

How did I remove every hidden block from my life allowing a free-flowing abundance of all my desires to constantly amaze me?

How did I learn the secret of allowing so many amazing people to show up in my life every single day teaching me things that continue to make life more abundant, more enjoyable, more fulfilling, more satisfying and more gratifying?

How did I find all the keys in the Universe that revealed a secret world where there are no unfulfilled desires, no unfulfilled dreams?

How did I know that it was always my answers to my questions that allowed me to choose my experiences?

How was I always able to allow the flow of abundance of health, wealth and love into my life so easily every single moment of my life?

How did I discover that by freeing my mind of all false beliefs that this was the door to all my dreams becoming my realities?

How did I discover how to always be happy and feel good no matter what the conditions of my life were, which made all the conditions of life that much better?

ASKffirmations Is A Technique, A Method, Whereby You Create Your Reality by Way of Asking Yourself the Right Questions with The Specific Answer Already in The Question, And They Are Always Past Tense. They Are Thinking FROM the Wish Fulfilled Rather Than OF the Wish Fulfilled. It Is How You Ask That Determines Your Experience.

How did I discover the Master Key to all the doors to a better life, where others who said there are no doors had no access?

How was I suddenly able to perceive a world where the Thoughts I chose were expressed instantly?

How was I always able to maintain the weight I always held in my mind with such ease?

How was I always able to live life in perfect health without any extra effort?

How did I so easily master the ability to attract in my life anything I desired instantly?

How was I always able to realize all my dreams by asking myself specific questions with specific answers?

How was I suddenly able to create a youthful body and keep that youthful body my entire long, healthy life?

How did I discover all the secrets of mastering the Thoughts I think, which allowed me to master all the circumstances in my life?

How did I discover all the secrets of perfect health, which allowed me to live a full and rewarding life?

How did I discover the true meaning of Nikola Tesla's, "If you wish to understand the universe, think of energy, frequency and vibration" while sitting in the silence and thinking about it?

How did I discover all the different ways to ask my Subconscious Mind for my desires, so that all my desires would be fulfilled 100% of the time?

The Secret Is Knowing How to Ask.

How did I discover that by putting my own answer in my own questions that the Subconscious Mind would give me any experience I chose?

How did I discover the magic of words, which opened a whole new world in which to live my life, from then on?

How did I realize that everything I desired in life was born the moment I Thought about it and came into expression by simply giving thanks for it?

How did I discover that the Subconscious Mind withholds nothing from those who know how to ask?

How did I discover the secrets of my Subconscious Mind were revealed to me so that I could now communicate with it directly and have anything I desired?

How did I realize which words were most creative of what I chose to experience in life?

How did my questions keep getting better and better with every question I asked, which made every one of my experiences better than the last?

How was I always able to keep finding new and better ways to manifest the reality of my choosing?

How did I have all the answers to all my questions answered so easily by asking this question?

How did I discover that my Subconscious Mind goes to work immediately to bring me my desires because of the questions I asked with the answer already provided for it?

How was I suddenly able to discover my own secrets to manifesting everything I desired?

How did I MASTER my chosen profession in such a short time, so easily?

How did I become such a powerful MAGNET for everything I desire by asking this question?

ASKffirmations Are ALWAYS Past Tense. The Works Are Done. The Wish Is Already Fulfilled. There Is Nothing Else to Do.

How did I reach that point so easily where I had an ever-increasing love for life that never left me?

How did I learn all the secrets to waking up every single day always feeling better than the previous day?

How did I end up with such an amazing and magical life by asking how did I end up with an amazing and magical life?

How did I discover that the better my questions were the better my life became?

How did I discover that the art and skill of asking the right questions were making me a master of creating my own experiences?

How did I uncover the most amazing ways to feel so good by just using better words?

How did I realize that by asking "How did I," rather than "How do I," that all my experiences were rapidly coming to me?

How did I discover that my questions opened an invisible portal within where all the answers to life exist and are always readily available?

How did my deep breathing improve every area of my life so easily and effortlessly?

How did I realize that I could enter any state-of-mind by asking how I entered that state-of-mind, which created all the great experiences that came from that state-of-mind?

How did I discover which questions would always give me the exact experiences I specifically chose as my reality?

How did my always feeling good every day cause such an abundance of prosperity, love and health to be my normal state-of-being for my entire life?

How did I discover my questions removed all obstacles from my path allowing me only the best experiences in life?

How did I discover that by sitting in the silence with no outer distractions that my creative questions were much more powerful?

You Choose the Question, You Choose the Answer, And the Experience Is Given unto You.

How did I know that by answering my own questions, I could convert any dream into a reality?

How did I realize that putting the answer of my choice into my question that the way would be made clear for me to realize my dreams?

How did I know that knowledge of the Subconscious Mind would give me the secret of creation?

How did I know that knowing the definitions of certain words would make me a better conscious creator?

How did I know that my Subconscious Mind is the Genie that grants all my wishes?

How did I so easily become a deliberate creator of my experiences and conditions of my life?

How did I realize I could fill up my life with an abundance of wealth, health, love and all things good with nothing more than thinking, speaking and writing that I already had all these things?

How did I know that by eliminating certain words from my vocabulary that I would eliminate from my life the conditions and experiences that those words created?

How was I able to make my natural state-of-being in all areas of my life ease and flow and peace-of-mind by refusing to use words such as ... want, need, wish, crave, desire, demand, lack, hope, etc. ... following "I"?

How did I free myself from unwanted feelings with nothing more than eliminating from my vocabulary the words that created those feelings?

How did I figure out how extremely important it is to my well-being to know that what I was adding to my "I" and "I AM" had to be spoken upward and never downward to secure increasingly better-quality results?

How did I know that investing my time in learning the language of deliberate creation it would give me a magical life?

If an Answer to YOUR Question Doesn't Feel Right, Then It's Not YOUR Answer. Choose A Better Answer.

How did I realize that by being positive in all areas of my life, inspiration would always come easy to me?

How did I know that by eliminating certain words from my vocabulary that I would eliminate the conditions and experiences that those words created from having any influence in my life?

How did I attract so many amazing friends into my life by using better words to communicate with myself?

How did I discover all the words to use that made all my dreams come true?

How did I realize that I could choose my reality by choosing what to agree or not to agree to?

How did I know that to get to the truth of what it means to be a creator, that the best method was to ask questions on how to get to the truth of what it means to be a creator?

How did I know the best way to improve my life was to ask questions on how to improve my life and give my own answers?

How did I know that feeling love for anything in life would increase love in all areas of my life by making love my natural state of being?

How did I know how vitally important it is to give my attention only to those things in life that lifted me to greater heights, which gave me greater experiences and conditions?

How did I discover that Thought was the Creator of my life's experiences and conditions and that Thought is those words we speak, write or hear in the silence of our mind, and that my Thought becomes my reality?

How did I realize that to create the best reality I desired I had to choose only the best things in life to agree to?

How did I recognize that by acknowledging and appreciating daily the blessings and love already in my life that the blessings and love in my life would increase exponentially?

How did I discover that by sitting in the silence and quieting the noise from the outer world, that more insight into how I could better my life would come into my conscious mind allowing me to make better choices in all areas of my life?

Discover the Principles of Mind for Yourself and Transform Your Life by Applying Them.

How did I open a portal for an abundance of love, health and wealth to enter my life allowing me to get the most out of life for myself and others?

How did I realize the immense power that the words I chose to speak had everything to do with how my life played out?

How did I bless myself with words, which allowed me to bless others with words, which allowed this to indefinitely bless people throughout the world making the world a better place for all to exist in?

How did I discover that by saying the words, "Thank You" every time something good happened in my life, I was causing more good things to happen in my life?

How did I discover that The Power of I AM was the power to make miracles happen?

How did I know that the power and influence that an agreement in mind had was allowing a condition or experience into my life, and without that agreement the condition or experience could not come into my life?

How did my questions reveal a new heaven and a new earth that remains hidden to those who have not discovered the power of their own words?

How did I become so aware of my words, that I only spoke those words that allowed into my experience only the best things that life had to offer?

How did I realize that to better my life I could do it with Thoughts only?

How did I discover the very best way to ask questions was to first choose the reality I desired, put it into question form, FROM the wish fulfilled and then live from that consciousness, of already having my desire?

How did I know that my own words could imprison me, and my own words could free me?

How did I discover that creation takes place in consciousness and is externalized as my reality by my Subconscious Mind?

The ANSWER Is The QUESTION. The EXPERIENCE Is The Result.

How did I eliminate the need for competition, to have everything in life I desired, by simply having the consciousness of already possessing my desires?

How did I discover that all the secrets of imagining my desires from the wish fulfilled were the key to get any experience I chose in life?

How did I know that investing my time in understanding words that it would be the greatest investment I would ever make in life?

How was I able to so easily master all aspects to my chosen profession in such a short period of time?

How did I know that by understanding the laws of creation, the laws of words, the laws of consciousness, that there was never a need to turn to another to create any part of my reality?

How did I remove all obstacles from my life using words, which opened a door for all I desired to enter unobstructed, with nothing more than the right use of words?

How did I discover the easiest way to control my Thoughts was to believe I could, which allowed me to control my life?

How did I learn to control my feelings 100% of the time by realizing my words created my feelings?

How did I discover which feelings created health, which feelings created wealth, which feelings created love and from that day on all these things were always present in my life because I only lived with those feelings?

How did I know that I didn't have to agree to anything, whether it was true or not, if I was to consciously choose my own reality?

How did I know that by taking my conscious attention away from all negative aspects of life that a door would open to a bigger, brighter, more loving world, than I could have ever imagined?

How did I know that to stop thinking certain Thoughts all I had to do was stop talking about them and they would go away all on their own?

Your Answer Determines Your Experience.

How did I learn all the secrets of love, which made my life a magical paradise filled with love?

How did I learn all the secrets of wisdom, which showed me how to do anything in life I chose?

How was I able to master all the secrets to wealth that have always been known only to the few by sitting in the silence?

How was I able to master all the secrets to health that have been hidden from the mind of man for centuries?

How was I able to master all the secrets to love that have eluded most of mankind by simply thinking I already had them?

How did I discover all the right secrets to accomplish anything my heart desired?

How did I know my answers were creating my life and that no other answers mattered?

How did I learn the secret language of words?

How did I learn how to quiet my mind so easily by speaking to it?

How did I learn to attract any person I desired into my life by asking, "How did I attract this person so easily into my life"?

How did I know that positive words created a positive life, and negative words created a negative life?

How did I so easily let go of past negative feelings, which ushered in a new and better life?

 How did I discover that saying, "Thank You," even if it was for no reason at all, would cause good things to happen in my life?

How did I realize the power of making my last Thoughts of the day ones of gratitude, appreciation and thankfulness were the secrets that filled my life with blessings?

Look Closely. The Answer Is in The Question Which Then Reveals the Experience.

How did I learn that life was always giving me what I asked for and that I could ask for anything?

How was I always able to manifest every single one of my desires by knowing that the secret of manifestation was to ask?

How did I make creation so easy by always knowing what to think?

How did my constant Thoughts of abundance for all things good always create so much abundance in my life so easily?

How did I suddenly become super aware of just how powerful my Thoughts were to create the reality of my choosing?

How did I realize that the enjoyment I got out of life was always within the power of my Thoughts and not anything in the without?

How did I accomplish so many things that have never been done before by anyone?

How did I finally come to the realization that my Thoughts were all powerful in creating any reality I chose, which removed all Thoughts of having to take any action to create?

How did I know the secret of always being in control of my feelings was always within my Thoughts, no matter what conditions were?

How did I discover The Truth That Sets Us Free?

How did I become so conscious of my words that I was able to create a life that dreams are made of?

How did I know that for me to have all my desires, *how* I asked was just as important as *what* I asked for?

How did I remove all doubt from my mind, which allowed me to create any condition that I desired in my life, anytime I desired?

How did I know that the reason I had no limitations in life was because I had no limitations in my mind?

When You See the Principle of ASKffirmations, When You Understand How They Work, Why They Work, You Are in Possession of Something So Great You Will Wonder Why or How You Never Knew It Before.

How did I free my mind from all negativity, which removed all negative conditions from my life from that day forward?

How did I fill my mind with so much positivity that an abundance of positive things happened from that day forward?

How did I discover that to manifest all my desires the biggest thing to remove from my life was doubt in what I was always telling myself?

How did I realize that there is no fiction, and that what I continually put before my mind was being created as experiences in my life?

How was I able to magically create the life I always dreamed about by discovering the power of my own words?

How did I realize my Subconscious Mind was my Genie and my Thoughts were my 'wishes'?

How did I always have so much more energy by just being positive?

How did I know that my questions were manifesting my reality faster than any other method I have ever used?

How did I know that by choosing my own answers I was choosing my own reality?

How did I know that my positive Thoughts (silent, spoken or written) were always creating positive things, conditions, experiences and circumstances in my life?

How did I know that it was my Thoughts (silent, spoken or written) that were the only magic I needed to make all the dreams I was seeking come true?

Your Words to Self Are Magical. See the Magic in Them. There Is Power in Your Words.

How did I realize that my Thoughts, whether silent, written or spoken were literally creating my reality?

How did my Thoughts become so powerful and magnetic that I was able to manifest anything I chose, instantly?

How did I discover and know that my questions were creative of conditions and experiences and not just of seeking answers and explanations?

How did I know that something as simple as using different words was responsible for giving me a different and better reality?

How did I realize that by acknowledging the good already in my life, being grateful for what I already had, giving thanks for what I already had, and appreciating what I already had, I was drawing an abundance of more good things into my life?

How did I know that it is not just asking better questions that is important, but that my experiences are determined by *how* I ask?

How was I able to know the difference between asking questions FROM the wish fulfilled rather than OF the wish fulfilled that was determining my reality?

How did I know the difference between asking, "How *do* I?" and asking, "How *did* I?" was giving me completely different results in my life?

How did I learn to ask the most amazing questions to get the most amazing experiences life has to offer?

How did I know the difference between asking a question with my answer already in it and asking a question seeking an answer was creating two different realities?

How did I know that I could use words and nothing more to feel anything I chose to feel?

How did I realize that by expressing my joy for life every single day that the joy for life would spring up from within me like a well of living water?

How did I discover the only way to always feel good was to keep saying 'I Feel Good' every single day?

The Secret to A Happy Life Is to Speak It into Existence.

How did I discover that by associating with other positive people that my positiveness would increase 10-fold, 10 times faster than by trying to be positive on my own without associating with them?

How did I know that my giving my constant attention to anything was asking for that thing to be in my life?

How did I know that the quality of my questions and the quality of my answers made the quality of my experiences what they were?

How did I become so successful using the Power of Positive Thought?

How did I learn all the secrets to making life magical?

How did I discover that there is, in fact, a secret language of the Subconscious Mind, and that by my giving all my attention to learning this language, I became more and more aware of it until I mastered it?

How did I realize that the reason my answers to my questions felt so good is because I was, in fact, creating the experience as I was thinking and giving birth to the experience within, so that it could have expression in the world without?

How did I know my inner conversations were the very beginning of what would always end up as my outer experiences, and that by controlling these inner conversations, I was controlling my outer experiences?

How did I discover that there were secrets to words that the definitions of those words didn't reveal, and those secrets revealed an entirely new and better world in which I live?

How did I learn to master words so quickly that I was able to think only what I wanted to think and create any reality I wanted to create anytime I wanted to create it?

How did I learn all the creative words that opened the windows of Heaven, which poured out all its gifts and rewards on me?

How did I know that my peaceful Thoughts were responsible for creating my peace of mind?

Make the Question and Answer Give You What You Ask For (The Experience)!

How did I discover that whatever I added to "I", or "I AM" was always added as an experience in my life?

How did my life always continue to get better and better with each passing moment once I increased my knowledge of the laws of Thought and applied them?

How did I accomplish my financial freedom so easily with nothing more than positive thinking?

How did my positive thinking create such financial abundance in my life?

How did I acquire financial freedom with nothing more than filling my mind with prosperous Thoughts?

How did I know that by knowing the definition of certain words, it was filling in the holes that many teachings left out of the Law of Attraction, making it easier to always secure the results I was seeking?

How did my always thinking of prosperous words, prosperous ideas and prosperous stories create a such windfall of prosperity in my life?

How did my always thinking of health-related words, health-related ideas and anything related to health, cause me to always be in perfect health?

How did my always thinking of the word Love, always affirming the word Love and always giving my attention to all things to do with Love, bring such an abundance of Love into my life all the time?

How did my only using positive words in my Thought (silent, spoken or written) cause an avalanche of positive things to always happen to me in abundance?

How did my only using positive words to communicate with myself and others reveal all the secrets of attracting the best of everything in life to me all the time?

How did I know that always thinking "I Feel Good" (silent, spoken or written) was the source of my *always* feeling good?

How did I know that the source of all good things in my life came from the words I chose to use?

Seek the Right Question with The Fulfillment of Your Desire as Your Answer, Which You Insert in The Question and The Result Is Your Experience.

It Works.

How did my always being super aware of my self-talk, my inner conversations, reveal to me the secrets of a happy, successful, healthy life always filled with loving people?

How did I learn that by using the right words I was in control of my own destiny?

How did my focusing on words such as prosperity, health, love, wisdom, harmony, freedom, joy, serenity, and peace reveal a life of constant satisfaction that is only revealed to those who think of these things?

How did I know that whatever I added to my I AM, was responsible for what came into my life?

How did I know that by waking up every day with such a positive attitude that I was causing an avalanche of positive things to happen in my life 24/7/365?

How did I know that the source of anything that happened in my life was my very own words (silent, spoken or written)?

How did my saying," I AM Blessed" every day reveal to me that I have always been able to bless myself with just those words (silent, spoken or written)?

How did I have all the secrets of health revealed to me by just meditating on the word, Health, while in the silence?

How did I know that filling my mind with prosperous Thoughts all the time that they were the seeds of a prosperous life?

How did I finally realize the secret of what meditation is and what it does for me?

How did I discover the Secret of Creation by sitting in the silence and meditating on what the Secret of Creation was until it was revealed to me from within?

Life, Mind, The Universe, Reflects to The Thinker What the Thinker Thinks.

How did I have all the secrets to life revealed to me by always looking within and waking up to the true cause of all that befalls me?

How did my always taking time to sit in the silence reveal to me the immense value of sitting in the silence?

How did I discover the secret of how my words were creating my reality, whether silent, spoken or written?

How did I learn that the secret of happiness was to always think happy Thoughts and stop thinking any Thoughts that weren't making me feel happy, including not giving my attention to or reacting to anything, or responding to anything or anyone who is not in alignment with all things to do with happiness?

How did I learn that the secret of getting a specific experience was to make my question give me the experience by my answering my own question FROM the wish fulfilled?

How did I have the secret revealed to me that my experiences have their beginning in my words, (silent, spoken or written)?

How did I have the secret of words revealed to me by meditating on what the secret of words were?

How did I realize the secret of obtaining all my chosen desires was to know how to use words, silent, spoken or written?

How did I know the secret of expression was in making the right impression with my words?

How did I realize that the very best time to ask myself questions to which I was seeking answers was just prior to sleep, and that as I slept, my Subconscious would give me the answer upon waking?

How did I know there is immense value in understanding what words I use daily and how they affect my life?

How did I know that I do truly create my reality, and I do it with Thoughts (silent, spoken or written)?

Always Ask FROM the Wish Fulfilled

How did I know that I could believe things true with nothing more than my words?

How did I know that the best answers tailored just for me would come to me as I sat in the silence pondering the questions and allowing the answers to come to me naturally?

How did my knowing what decree meant, meant that I could decree anything, and have it given to me?

81

How did I have more secrets to life revealed to me by believing that I would have more secrets to life revealed to me?

How did I have revealed to me the secret of finding the right answers for me was to believe that the right answers for me would be revealed to me?

How did I have revealed to me that the magic of believing in myself was the secret to having all things I desired?

How did I know that the secret of having all my dreams come true was to believe that all my dreams had already become true?

How did I know that my life was playing out according to my words ... to my I AM ... to my every Thought?

How did something so simple as believing in myself cause so many wonderful and amazing things to happen in my life?

How did I know how to use my imagination to create the most amazing life imaginable in the shortest span of time imaginable?

How did I know that always speaking to others using positive words would evoke positive responses out of them, causing positive things to happen in my life by creating a positive atmosphere for them to be attracted to me?

How did I know that the secret of Love was in first Loving myself and then all Love would be drawn to me automatically as I contemplated what Love meant to me?

How did I discover the secrets of peace-of-mind were being revealed to me from within as I retreated into the silence and quieted the chatter of the outer world and meditated on peace of mind?

We Think into This Mind and It Is Given unto Us... Just What We Thought into It. This Mind Is Unlimited! Do Not Hesitate to Ask for The Best.

How did I discover the secrets of meditation by going into the silence and mediating on what the secrets of meditation were?

How did I discover that any secret I desired to know was as simple as asking myself the question, "How did I learn the secret to that?" ... and then allowing the secret to be revealed to me as my harvest from within?

How did I discover that the Subconscious Mind was continually revealing to me from within how to communicate with it, which allowed me to have all my desires granted?

How did I learn all the secrets, mysteries and powers of the Subconscious Mind by asking the Subconscious Mind what all its secrets, mysteries and powers were?

How did I discover that the secret of an abundantly prosperous life was to only use abundantly prosperous words?

How did I discover the secret of an abundantly healthy life was to only speak of being abundantly healthy?

How did I discover exactly how my Thoughts create my reality?

How did I discover the secret of always having all my desires fulfilled instantly was to understand how my Thoughts created them?

How did I become so fluent in communicating with my Subconscious Mind that everything I desired showed up in my life in record time?

How did I know that I could feel any feeling I wanted to feel by adding that feeling to the words, "I Feel," such as "I Feel Good"?

How did I know that one of the most important things in life was to know exactly how my Thoughts were creating my reality?

How did I know that the power of my Thoughts was responsible for anything I desired in life?

How did I discover all the mysteries of life by asking how did I know all the mysteries of life?

Your Mind Is More Powerful Than You Have Ever Been Taught. Now You Are Awake to The Power of Your Thoughts. Create Wisely and Consciously.

How did I know that how to get rid of any unwanted feeling was by ignoring the unwanted feeling and replacing it with, "I Feel Great" or "I Feel Good" until those new feelings consumed my conscious mind?

How did it become so easy for me to manifest my desires by believing I could easily manifest my desires?

How did I make every single day of my life a magical paradise to live in with nothing more than my own magical words?

How did I discover that my words were magical and that I could produce any desired effect in my life by simply realizing this and speaking magical words?

How did I discover that the key to a happy, successful life was to say that I have a happy, successful life?

How did I discover that my words were the only magical potion I needed to make of my life anything I desired?

How did I know that the more attention I gave to my words being magical, the more magical they became to me?

How did I discover all the secrets of words by asking how did I know all the secrets of words?

How did I discover all the powers of words by asking how did I know all the powers of words?

How did I discover all the secrets of consciousness by asking consciousness to reveal all the secrets of consciousness to me?

How did I discover that all the secrets to life were to realize I already had all the secrets to life?

How did I know that my own personal Genie was my Subconscious Mind and that my Genie gave me everything I asked for?

There Is Nothing to Do but Ask with The Answer in The Question. That Is the Only Action You Take. Life Will Do the Rest. Always Ask FROM the Wish Fulfilled.

How did I always know just the right questions to ask to get any desire I asked for when I asked for it?

How did I know exactly how to use my imagination to create any desired condition in my life any time I chose to?

How did I learn the secret of making any word magical that I chose to make magical by knowing that I could make any word magical?

How did I reveal all the secrets of consciousness to the world by asking consciousness to reveal all its secrets to the world?

How did I realize I could talk to anyone, living or dead, by speaking to them in consciousness and having them inspire me to greater heights in the magic of creation?

How did I realize saying, "I Feel Good" every single day of my life erased all negative feelings I have ever had and wouldn't let them return to me ever again?

How did I realize that the faith I had in my own words was what supercharged them with more magical power?

How did I know one of the biggest secrets to a healthy life was in taking time to deep breathe every single day?

How did I know that by speaking to the cells in my body with love and positivity that they would respond back with perfect health?

How did I know the secret of having Love in my life was to have Love for all things in my consciousness every single day?

How did I know the secret of the right answer was in asking the right question?

How did I know that I could have anything in existence bless me by asking it to bless me?

How did I discover all the secrets of creation by asking creation to reveal all its secrets to me?

How was it always so easy for me to always ask the right questions that always gave me all my desires?

How did I suddenly start receiving an influx of large sums of money from multiple sources by simply asking this question?

ASKffirmations Give You The Consciousness Of Already Possessing Your Desire.

How did I know that I could have wealth reveal all its secrets to me by asking it to reveal all its secrets to me?

How did I know that I could have health reveal all its secrets to me by asking it to reveal all its secrets to me?

How did I know that I could have wisdom reveal all its secrets to me by asking it to reveal all its secrets to me?

How did I know that I could have knowledge reveal all its secrets to me by asking it to reveal all its secrets to me?

How did I know that I could have Love reveal all its secrets to me by asking it to reveal all its secrets to me?

How did I discover the secret of magnetizing myself to attract only the best of everything in life?

How did I know that to get rid of one Thought I didn't like all I had to do was replace it with a better Thought the moment I had that unwanted Thought, and if that other Thought persisted, all I had to do was keep repeating my new Thought until the old Thought just gave up?

How did I discover all the mysteries of consciousness by believing I had already solved all the mysteries of consciousness?

How did I discover all the secrets of how our minds work by realizing I had already solved all the secrets of how our minds work?

How did I discover that the secret of always getting my desires was in how I used my WORDS?

How did I discover that it is WORDS that bless people?

How did I realize that it was WORDS that set us free from any condition in the world?

How did I discover that it is WORDS that light our path to any destination we strive to get to in life?

Awaken to The Power of Your Own Thoughts. You Control Your Life, The Things You Speak, The Way You Feel. You Are the Captain of Your Life.

How did I discover that it is WORDS that reveal to us anything we desire in life?

How did I discover that it is WORDS that make us healthy, make us wealthy, and bring love into our lives?

How did I discover which WORDS revealed all the secrets to Love?

How did I know that I can talk to WORDS and have WORDS reveal their secrets to me?

How did I discover that it is my WORDS that determined 100% of my feelings no matter what conditions were or are in my life?

How did I discover that as my WORDS improved my health improved?

How did I realize that my finances improved as my WORDS improved?

How did I discover that I could solve any mystery of mind or consciousness by not considering it as, or calling it, a mystery?

How did I discover that by using more loving WORDS, I was filling my consciousness with more and more love, and this one act was causing more love to spill into my life?

How did I discover that WORDS were the source of my feelings and nothing else?

How did I discover that every time I Thought of the word LOVE, I was planting a SEED of love into my consciousness, and this was responsible for more love coming into my life?

How did I discover that negative words governed my life negatively and positive words governed my life positively?

How did I discover that asking myself any question about feeling negative was perpetuating my feeling negative?

Asleep to The Power of Thoughts You Are Vulnerable to Suggestions from Sources Outside of Your Own Consciousness. Awake and Aware, You Control Your Own Destiny.

How did I discover that the more positive WORDS I used (silent, spoken or written) I was improving the quality of my life more than any other thing in life could have ever done?

How did I know that I was allowing answers to my questions to come to me by believing I already had the answers?

How did I know that I was giving permission for conditions and experiences to happen to me by giving my attention to them?

How did I know my WORDS were my wishes and that they were self-fulfilling?

How did I know that I was inviting experiences into my life by believing they were already my experiences?

How did I know that WORDS are alive and that by my thinking them (silent, written or spoken), I was activating them and giving them permission to perform the actions for which they were given life by me?

How did I know not to ask any question which was intended to solicit an answer, but to already have my answer and put it in question form, which then revealed to me what the outer experience or condition would be, thereby giving it to me as an experience or condition?

How did I know that feeling good was not just a feeling, but a vibration that magnetized me, which attracted to me everything I desired?

How did I discover that the Fountain of Youth was my own Thoughts (silent, spoken or written) and that by living life FROM a mindset of being perpetually youthful, I was causing youth to be my natural state of being?

How did I know that whatever I add to "I Feel" was asking for that feeling, and whatever I asked for was given unto me?

Do Not Accept Anything as True About Your Life That You Do Not Desire to Be True. You Are A Creator. You Decide What Is True for You. What You Allow to Be Your Reality. The Outer World Will Cease to Have Any Negative Effect on You.

How did I discover the most amazing way to have love come to me was to always think loving Thoughts, which magnetized for me for an abundance of love to flow into my life?

How did I know that by only focusing on the best in life, only the best in life would be drawn to me?

How did I know that by simply thinking of health-related words I was generating more health every day?

How did I realize that the longer I held an idea in consciousness the more secrets would be revealed to me on how to make that idea an even better reality than I had imagined?

How did I realize that I was constructing my life without by the Thoughts I was thinking all day long, and the more creative my Thoughts were the better my life became?

How did I realize that by talking to my Thoughts as though they were living beings they would do things for me that living beings would do for me had I asked them?

How did I know that I was becoming more and more successful with each positive Thought I had and that any negative Thought I had was holding me back from success?

How did I know that every word I used in communicating with myself was related to the word, success, and I was creating more success with each word?

How did I realize that everything in life held secrets and that all those secrets would be revealed to me as I claimed them in consciousness?

How did I know that Thought was the Magic Wand that had always been creating everything in my life?

How did I know that my Subconscious Mind was my own personal Genie and that as I decreed anything in consciousness, it was given to me?

How did I know that success is a state-of-mind that spills over into the conditions and experiences of my life?

How did I know that I could always get a great night's sleep, waking up refreshed and full of energy, by always saying, "I always get a great night's sleep and wake up feeling refreshed and full of energy"?

You Create Your Reality by The Thoughts You Think, By the Questions You Ask, By What You Accept as True, By What You Give Your Attention To, By What You Focus On, By What You Believe. Create the Best Life Possible. There Are No Limits to What You Can Do When You Understand Thoughts. Only Speak What You Desire.

How did I know that I could feel excitement with nothing more than always saying, "I AM excited"?

How did I know that by simply meditating on the word, Success, often throughout the day, every day, that I was creating the blueprint for success in my consciousness and that my Subconscious Mind was making me more aware of the opportunities all around me, day in and day out, which made me successful at everything I did?

How did I know that I could always feel satisfied under all conditions by saying, "I AM always satisfied"?

How did I know that I could always have fun by always saying, "I AM always having fun"?

How did I know that I could increase my energy by always saying, "My energy is always increasing"?

How did I know that I could awaken to a greater life by always saying, "I AM awakening to a greater life"?

How did I know that I could be free from all negativity affecting my life by saying, "I AM free from all negativity affecting my life"?

How did I know that I could always bless others by always saying, "I AM always blessing others"?

How did I know the secret of happiness was to always say, "I AM Happy"?

How did I know that I could fill up my life with an abundance of all things good by saying, "My life is always filling up with all things good"?

How did I know that by always saying, "I Feel Good," I was always feeling good?

How did I know that always having peace-of-mind was as simple as always saying, I have peace-of-mind"?

You Choose. It's Always A Choice. Don't Accept Anything Less Than the Best Thoughts and You'll Have Nothing but The Best Experiences.

How did I know that I could always have the solution to anything by always saying, "I always have the solution to everything'?

How did I know that I could always feel relaxed by always saying, "I AM always relaxed"?

How did I know that I could always feel content by always saying, "I AM always content"?

How did I know that the cells in my body have always been responding to my Thoughts, and that as I improved my Thoughts, my health improved?

How did I know that to keep improving my memory, all I had to do was keep saying, "My memory is always improving"?

How did I discover freedom from all conditions by always saying, "I AM free from all conditions?"

How did I know that to keep increasing my income, all I had to do was keep saying, "My income is always increasing"?

How did I know that to always have amazing experiences in life, all I had to do was keep saying, "I AM always having amazing experiences in life"?

How did I know that to always have all my dreams come true, all I had to do was keep saying, "All my dreams are always coming true"?

How did I know that the best way for me to always feel rejuvenated was to always say, "I AM always rejuvenated?"

How did I know that I could always have secrets to anything in life revealed to me by always saying, "I AM always having revealed to me secrets to all things in life"?

How did I know that I could talk to the cells in my body, thank them for all they do for me and have them show appreciation by always giving me better health?

How did I discover the secret of always having great things come into my life was to always say, "Great things are always coming into my life"?

You Are Creating What You are Thinking. The Coin of Heaven Is Your Thoughts, Either Silent, Spoken or Written. You Pay for Experiences with Your Own Words.

How did know that I could receive love and inspiration from anyone living or dead by believing that anyone living, or dead was sending me love and inspiration?

How did I awaken all the latent powers of my mind by continually saying, "I have awakened all the latent powers of my mind"?

How did I know that the Subconscious Mind would reveal all its secrets to me because I was always telling myself that the Subconscious Mind was always revealing all its secrets to me?

How did I know that I could remain youthful my entire life by always telling myself that I have always been youthful my entire life?

How did I discover that to increase anything in life, all I had to do was keep affirming the things I desired to increase until the things I affirmed naturally increased?

How did I discover that one of the best ways to learn anything was to believe that I had already learned it and to keep thinking that until what I had desired to learn had naturally come to me without any effort on my part?

How did I awaken all the latent and potential powers in my mind to accomplish any and all deeds I set out to accomplish in life?

How did I stimulate my Subconscious Mind to be more responsive to my exact desires by appreciating all it does for me?

How did I discover the easiest way to use 100% of my brain was to arouse it into activity by being grateful for and appreciating all that it does for me?

How did I know that the more positive I became, the more I was encouraging constructive Thoughts to be drawn into my mind, which allowed me to be more productive?

How did I know how to be blissful every second of my life by always saying, "I AM always blissful"?

How did I discover that my dreams were nothing more than Thoughts, and that the more exciting I made my Thoughts, the better my feelings became, and the better all my experiences in life became because of those feelings?

Words Are Magic.

How did I know that by always saying, "I Love Life," that I was creating a Life that I truly Loved?

How did I know the more I loved myself, the more love I would receive from others?

How did I know I could attract anyone into my life by continually feeling gratitude and appreciation for them every time I Thought about them?

How did I discover the added power of attraction that I possessed, by frequently telling myself, "I love myself"?

How was I always able to receive inspiration from everyone by believing I was always receiving inspiration from everyone?

How was I able to always think just what I had to think to create just what I desired to create?

How did I discover all the right words that created all the right feelings to create any condition I desired to create?

How did I discover the secret of deliberate creation was in feeling a deep appreciation for whatever it was that I desired?

How did I discover the secret world of vibrations that opened up a whole new world of experiences for me?

How was I able to have any word reveal its secrets to me by feeling that the word had already revealed all its secrets to me?

Speak Only What You Desire to Be True ... Because You are Making It True by Saying It and Believing It.

How did I know that my appreciation for anything was the magnet that brought the thing to me?

How did I keep awakening to a higher level of consciousness by always being more aware that I was always awakening to a higher level of consciousness?

How did I know that I was blessing myself by giving thanks and gratitude in advance for anything I desired to come into my life?

How did I realize that the more I appreciated anything, the more power I was given to attract it into my life?

How did I realize that the more I appreciated money, I was allowing more of an influx of money to come into my life?

How did I realize that the more I appreciated anything, I was opening a channel for that thing to come freely into my life?

How did I realize that my answers to my own questions were me giving birth to my outer experiences?

How did I know that acknowledging the good that is already in my life was one of the things responsible for bringing even more good things into my life?

How did I know that gratitude is the attitude that opened up a portal, where magic and dreams happen, every second of every day?

How did I know that feeling love, joy, excitement, gratitude and appreciation for anything in life was me magnetizing myself to draw more of the same to me?

How did I become awake to my imaginative powers, which revealed a world where all my dreams came true?

How did I know that my always saying, "I Feel Good," was me giving birth to my always feeling good, and that by saying it every day, I was nurturing it into my natural state of being?

How did I know that in order to experience the feeling of always loving life, all I had to do was keep saying, "I Love Life," every single day?

How did I know that it was my words that made me feel good and not conditions?

The Power is IN the Words You Speak. Every Time You Speak, You Are Asking.

How did I finally realize just how creative my words were in creating my life?

How did I know that WORDS become Things?

How did I know that WORDS create Reality?

How did I learn that to feel good, *all* I had to do was *say*, "I Feel Good"?

How did I discover the *astonishing* and *magical power* of asking questions to create my dreams, that all I had to do was start with the WORDS "How *did* I ..." and adding the wish fulfilled as my answer?

How did I discover the magic of the word, "I", to grant me my every desire?

How did I realize that three simple words, "How *did* I," were my magical Genie that granted me my every desire?

How did I know that my imagination was nothing more than my Thoughts and as I Thought what I wanted to think, I created what I wanted to create?

How did I discover so many new words and new ideas that opened up an entirely new world for me in which to exist?

How did I discover the secret of having my Subconscious Mind *only* give me my desires and nothing else?

How did I discover the secret of always and only getting the best of everything out of life?

How did I discover *all* the secrets of making wealth my permanent state of affairs?

How did I know the secret of creation was in knowing how to ask?

How did I know that an affirmation is asking for that thing that is affirmed?

Don't Concern Yourself with Feeling what You Speak. Say Anything Long Enough and You WILL Feel It. Your Words Are Creating the Feeling.

How did I know that giving my attention to anything was one form of asking for that thing?

How did I know that thinking of a thing and giving thanks for it was the same as asking for it?

How did I discover all the secret ways to ask for anything in life?

How did I discover the secret of always attracting the most amazing people into my life?

How did I discover the secret words for always attracting money into my life?

How did I discover the secret words for always experiencing perfect health?

How did I discover the secret words that always attracted the most loving people into my life?

How did I free myself from ever allowing any condition to ever have any negative effect on me ever again?

How did I discover the secret of always attracting whatever it was that I needed … when I needed it … to do whatever it was I needed it to do … was to ask for it?

How did I discover that I was blessed with the fulfillment of every single one of my desires by realizing I was blessed with the fulfillment of every single one of my desires?

How did I get so good at forming questions that all the answers I ever desired to know were revealed to me with no further effort on my part than to ask the questions?

How did I discover that I was blessing myself with the fulfillment of my desires by giving thanks to my desires for coming into my life before they even appeared to my senses?

How did I realize that by simply being more consciously aware of my breath that I was breathing better and improving my health at the same time?

How did I know there was a higher meaning to words than has been disclosed to mankind, and those higher meanings disclosed to me a higher existence where the magic of life happens?

Create Only the Best Feelings and You Will Have Only the Best Experiences.

How did my believing in the magic of words make words my own magic wand for creating any desire for which I asked?

How did I know that in order to get rid of a condition, all I had to do was get rid of the Thoughts that created and maintain the condition?

How did I know that I could ask my WORDS to do
things for me and they would do just what I asked
them to do?

How did I know that my words become the people in my
life, and that the better my words were, the better were
the people that came into my life?

How did I know that I could phrase a question and
produce the experience by asking myself the question
and giving myself the answer?

How did I know that, by my living in a state of
appreciation every day, I was making myself a stronger
magnet for all my desires to appear that much quicker?

How did life become so much more joyful the more I
Thought of the word, Joy?

How did everything I do in life become so much easier
the more I Thought of the word, Easy?

How did I know that the more positive I kept my state-
of-mind the more blessings I would create in my life?

How did I continually get the circumstances in my life to keep improving every single day of my life by simply acknowledging that the circumstances of my life were improving every single day of my life?

How did I finally realize all the powers of mind that have always been latent only needed my belief to become activated?

How did my life become so prosperous with such ease by my thinking of the word, Prosperity, all the time?

How did I realize that, as I put my ideas down in writing from the wish fulfilled, the words themselves were all that was needed to make all my dreams come true?

Why Does Asking, "How Did I ..." Create Our Experiences? Because it Gives Us the Consciousness of Already Possessing Our Desires, Which is the Impression, Which then Causes the Expression.

How did I know that the more I Thought of the word, Money, that this was the secret of money showing up in my life in unlimited and unexpected ways?

How did I know that the more I saw the good in people
the more good people were showing up in my life?

How did I discover that I was able to make life exciting
every single day by thinking of the word, Excitement, all
the time?

How did I realize that by meditating on one word that all
things related to that word were being drawn
into my experience?

How did I know that my thinking of the word, Love, that
all things associated with Love were being drawn
tome, effortlessly?

How did I know that by thinking of the words, Love,
Health or Wealth, and saying, "Thank You" after each
word, I was making the substance of these words take
form in my life?

How did I know that thinking of the words, Thank You,
I was increasing my vibration and making desires
manifest in my life so much quicker?

David Allen - ASKffirmations

How did I know that the secret of having words do things for me was to believe in the words?

How did I know that, as I Thought of the word, Vibrant, I was making my life more vibrant?

How did I know that, by thinking of the word, Luxury, I was bringing more and more luxurious things into my life without having to make any extra effort to do so?

How did I realize that, by thinking of the word, Paradise, every day, I was creating a paradise for me in which to exist?

End of ASKffirmations

Read YOUR ASKffirmations everyday and see for yourself how each time you read them they give you stronger and stronger feelings that they are becoming your external reality.

....

Create your own ASKffirmations

and see for yourself how magical they are for consciously creating your life.

Sample Format

Step 1: Identify your fulfilled desire.
- o Perfect Health

Step 2: Put it into question form, past tense (How did I).
- o How did I so easily get perfect health by asking this question?

Step 3: Read your question every day.
- o At least once-a-day (the more the better). The longer it stays in your conscious mind the more powerful it becomes in making it an external expression (in making it your reality). Each time you read it you can feel it getting stronger and stronger, which will be your sign that it is working.

Step 4: Let your Subconscious Mind make it your outer reality.
- o Allow the Subconscious to do its job. Your job is to know how to ask.

Remember: ASKffirmations do not merely seek an answer, unless that is what you desire. The point of an ASKffirmation is to give you the *consciousness of already having your desire*. That is the principle at work. For what you have in consciousness within is given to you as an expression without. When you have the consciousness of already having an answer, the expression is given unto you.

There is a science to mind. The more we know of this science the more we are able to consciously create our reality. Without knowledge of this science we are in the dark and must stumble along wishing, wanting, needing and hoping for things that are within our grasp once we understand the science of laws and principles and *apply* them.

Chapter Six

Questions Everyone Should Ask Themselves

As an additional tool, a companion to the ASKffirmations, I am proposing that you answer the following questions to bring an awareness to you of the more important aspects of being a creator. This includes The Law of Attraction, Metaphysics and Laws and Principles of Mind ... or basically, laws on how our lives work.

Revisit the questions from time to time. The longer they stay in your conscious mind, the more likely you are to receive your answers as you meditate or sit in the silence. As you receive your answers, you will realize just how easy it is to create your life using WORDS (Silent, Spoken or Written). Over time, you will experience new understanding and growth, which will assist you in living a better life.

Helpful Tip: *Use a notebook, write down your answers to these questions, date them, and look at them occasionally. You will be amazed at how at your growth and how much you are learning, understanding and changing your life for the better, all because of these questions to self that focus on creation. If you don't have an answer now, don't worry. The answers will come when you are ready for them.*

While it is not required to answer the questions below to be successful at ASKffirmations, working on them will increase your awareness as you continue to learn more about your own creative abilities.

Questions Everyone Should Ask Themselves

1. What does it really mean to be a creator?

2. How many different ways do we have at our disposal to create our reality?

3. Why is it important for me to answer my own questions?

4. Why is it important to re-read metaphysical books more than once, say every 3-6 months to a year for years to come?

5. What do I know about Thoughts creating my reality?

6. What do I know about the spoken word creating my reality?

7. What do I know about the written word creating my reality?

8. Why do I want to know more about being a creator of my own reality?

9. Why is it important to know that the within creates the without?

10. Why is it important to avoid all negativity from outside sources?

11. What does The Silence mean to me?

12. What does Meditation mean to me?

13. Why is it important to understand concentration?

14. Why is it important to understand focus?

15. Why is it important to understand suggestion and auto-suggestion?

16. Why is it important to understand awareness?

17. How do my Thoughts create my reality?

18. Why should I not react to negative situations?

19. Why should I be more aware of my own Thoughts?

20. Why are my inner conversations important?

21. What does imagination do?

22. How does imagining create reality?

23. Why does Neville Goddard say, "There Is No Fiction"?

24. What does Neville Goddard mean by "Consciousness is the only reality"?

25. What does Neville Goddard mean by "Assumptions Harden Into Fact"?

26. What does spiritual secrecy mean?

27. How important is it for me to know that I do, in fact, create my own reality?

28. Why is appreciation important to me, and what role does it play in my life?

29. Why is gratitude important to me, and what role does it play in my life?

30. Why is it important for me to feel good all the time?

31. Why are mantras an important aspect to my life?

32. Why is it important to know how my Thoughts affect my health?

33. How and why do my words affect the way I feel?

34. Do my Thoughts have anything to do with the way I age?

35. Why is it important for me to avoid all negativity?

36. Why is it important for me to not react to negativity?

37. Why should I only speak of positive things and aspects to life?

38. Why is it important for me to always go to sleep on a positive note?

39. Why should I ask myself questions, for which I am seeking answers, before I go to sleep?

40. Why are my answers to my own questions so important?

41. What is the best method I can use to overcome my negative thinking?

42. Why should I avoid negative thinking?

43. Which teachers of Metaphysics should I give my most attention to?

44. What does "Its Ways Are Past Finding Out" mean?

45. How much time should I invest in teaching myself the laws of being?

46. What are the most important Universal Laws?

47. How do Universal Laws affect my life?

48. What does Metaphysics mean to me?

49. Are some Universal Laws more important than others? Which ones are most important to me?

50. How important is it for me to look up dictionary definitions of metaphysical words?

51. What is the difference between looking for results and observing or being aware of results?

52. How important is it understand principles as they pertain to mind?

53. Why should I make my own list of my favorite metaphysical books?

54. Is it possible that in asking myself questions that the answers will come to me during meditation?

55. How important is interpretation of "these teachings" (anything metaphysical)?

56. Why should I trust my own interpretations, even if it is in agreement with others, who have interpreted them in a way that best suits me?

57. How long do I think it will take for me to understand what it means to be a creator?

58. Why are affirmations so beneficial to me?

59. Why should my focus be more on laws and principles than on money, health and love?

60. Should I tell others what I am planning to manifest?

61. Is it possible to learn about laws of mind in some other way than putting in the effort to study it myself?

62. When I do get a manifestation that I know I created, should I tell others?

63. Do I *really* believe that I know how The Law of Attraction works?

64. What role does what we are always telling ourselves play in our lives?

65. Why are my questions-to-self creative of my experiences?

66. Why is it important that I answer my own questions?

67. What new and amazing discoveries are awaiting my awareness of them?

68. Do I *really* understand that *my* words, not conditions, are creating the way I feel?

69. What would happen to my life if I looked at all negativity as a lie and all positivity as the truth?

70. If I knew that what I agreed to in life (believed to be true) was creating my reality, how much of what I believed, while I was asleep to this truth, would I change now that I am awake to this truth?

71. What would happen if I asked myself some questions but didn't attempt to give myself the answers, and let them come to me in meditation? What if I asked them so that the only way they could be answered was with, "Yes" as the answer? Is this a more creative process than other ways?

72. Is it really necessary to tell people what I am working to manifest?

73. Why is it important to know all the ways I can ask for something?

74. Why is it important to put metaphysical teachings to the test myself?

75. What are the limits of my imagination?

76. What does "In the Beginning Was the Word" mean?

77. Why is it important to take time each day to sit in the silence?

78. Why is it important for me to trust my own answers as opposed to trusting the answers that others give me?

79. Why do they call Thoughts "seeds"?

80. How important to me are my beliefs?

81. What does it mean to think FROM the end?

82. What is the difference between thinking OF the end and thinking FROM the end?

83. Why should I only speak about things I desire to see in my life?

84. What does "It is done unto us as we believe" mean?

85. Why should I only say things about myself that I desire to be true?

86. Why is it important to know as much about the Subconscious Mind as possible?

87. Can the Subconscious Mind be reprogrammed?

88. What are the different names that the Subconscious Mind has been called?

89. Where do my Thoughts come from?

90. Why should I avoid indulging in negative self-talk?

91. Why is it more important to focus on causes than effects?

92. Is it possible to control my Thoughts 100% of the time?

93. Why is it important to avoid using the words want, wish and need, when talking about my desires?

94. Can my Thoughts affect my health?

95. What does it mean to have a wealth consciousness?

96. What does it mean to have a health consciousness?

97. What does it mean that life is a mirror of our Thoughts?

98. How much time should I invest in understanding the laws of being?

99. Once I have obtained all my desires, can I then think whatever I want to think, and why or why not?

100. What does "The Truth Shall Set You Free" mean?

Add your own questions here. I have left a few blank pages if you choose to do so.

My Questions

My Questions

My Questions

Most of us are totally unaware of the mental activity which goes on within us. But to play the game of life successfully, we must become aware of our every mental activity, for this activity, in the form of inner conversations, is the cause of the outer phenomena of our life. - Neville Goddard

Chapter Seven

The POWER of WORDS

"In the Beginning Was the Word"

Sigmund Freud has been credited with saying...

"Words and magic were in the beginning one and the same thing, and even today words retain much of their magical power."

Words are still magic. The magic was never lost, only our knowledge and understanding of their magical power. It is my desire that this book restores that knowledge in the mind of man ... that by simply making more people aware, they will then gain the knowledge to transform their own lives by knowing how words do what they do. And with each person who becomes more aware, that knowledge will multiply and expand all over the world.

Words change lives. Words transform lives. Words *are* our lives.

So why doesn't everyone know this? Does that even matter? Is mankind simply realizing once again the magical power of words?

The purpose of this book is to provide information, to bring awareness into possibly the most important aspect of our lives, to bring more insight and understanding that can do for mankind more than perhaps any other teaching currently known to man ... to change and improve lives ... to change conditions in a person's life so much so that he will know beyond a shadow of a doubt that words are indeed as magical as they ever were.

I first become consciously aware of the power of words through reading hundreds of metaphysical books from the last 100 years or so. One of my first discoveries was The Power of I AM. Once I became aware of this Power, I started to watch my words very carefully from that day forward. I noticed immediately a change in how I felt. That was my introduction to the power of words in my own life. I knew then that I had found what was missing in my life ... a better understanding of words and what they could do.

Once I became more aware, I was then able to see in my reading that this knowledge had existed for a very long time. I could concentrate and focus on what was most important in my life, words.

What are words?

Words are our Thoughts. Words are silent, spoken and written. They are the substance of our lives. When we change the words we use, our lives reflect this change ... and that is power. The power is in our words. Words by themselves have no power, they are simply latent potential. Each of us activates our power by thinking words (silent, spoken or written). We are the operant power.

The WORD becomes flesh.

That means the words we speak (silent, spoken or written) become the people who show up in our lives, the conditions that form in our lives, the experiences that we have in life.

Words create.

Words create feelings. Words create moods. Words create ideas. Words inspire us. Words are the beginning of our actions. Words create conditions and experiences. The more we know about words and what they do, the better equipped we will be to make of our lives anything we desire.

Listen to your words. What are you always saying to yourself and others? Have you truly been aware of what you have been saying … of how it makes you feel? Do you really listen to your inner conversations? Are you aware that your inner conversations are the source of the coming attractions of your life? Why would it be otherwise?

Chapter Eight

Definitions of Key Words

One of my many discoveries in my studies of the Law of Attraction and metaphysics was to know definitions of certain words. While it could be debated that these definitions are referring to other aspects of life than the Law of Attraction, there is no reason why we should not to use our own imagination to see how they also relate to creation. The world is mostly asleep to our creative powers, and therefore it is not surprising that dictionaries would not include or refer to those powers in the definitions of many words.

See for yourself if they don't help you as well and notice how they do indeed apply to creation. Maybe one day someone will discover that the origin of some words was defining creation and that as time went on, the real significance was lost and given different worldly meanings, thereby burying the truth of how our lives really work, only to once again be discovered by those seeking higher meanings in today's world.

One thing we know for certain is that Thought is Creative.

However, shouldn't we ask ourselves exactly what Thought is... or means... so that we can know exactly how it is creative of the conditions and experiences in our lives? How would we go about finding out these things, so that we can create by design and not by default?

Each of us must decide what is true and what is not because what we ourselves say is true for us is how we create. So, the following information may prove valuable to those of you who are seeking more information on Thought. Let each of us decide for ourselves how creation works and share our findings with others who have the same desire to know.

A single word has the potential of making an entire concept understandable. If any of these words are not helpful, don't think they won't be down the road. Revisit these words often. You may be pleasantly surprised when one day, just one word will bring clarity to something you have been trying to understand, and the entire concept of being a creator will change, giving you the ability to turn all your dreams into realities.

Many of these words are synonyms of Thought.

Let's break down the definitions of these words, the ones that are most likely to apply to creation of our reality.

If you do not see the connection between these words and your creative powers of mind, don't concern yourself with them. There will come a time when you will see the connection, and it will improve your ability to be more deliberate in your creations when you are ready.

I believe the following definitions give the most insight into how our different uses of Thought are creative. I have also included other words that will provide clarity into the creative process. On the other hand, some words may explain how we create the opposite of what we desire to create.

A better understanding of words will give us a better understanding of how to create.

Let me add this. We are all creators of our life's experiences. The more we know about how our minds, consciousness, Thought, words, definitions, are always creating something, the better we will be able to create anything we desire. Without this knowledge and understanding, we would be living in the dark, leaving us wondering what we are doing wrong. These words will shed more light on this understanding.

Understanding WORDS helps us better understand CREATION.

Empower yourself by knowing every aspect of creation that you can possibly know.

Use your imagination to envision how these words could easily explain the act of creation. This may be one key that most metaphysical teachers haven't yet explored as a means for more people to understanding creation.

While those who have never considered themselves to be creators or who are new at being deliberate creators, these words would most likely hold only a worldly definition. Those who are awake to the creative powers that we all possess should now see that the very same words that others see as "worldly words" can be seen and associated with our creative powers.

Let's turn to some dictionaries for our definitions and look for the relationship between these definitions and creation. They may just hold the key that allows you to connect the dots between the things we say and the things we create in our lives.

This is from my morning awareness where I heard "ask Siri" to look up the word, "fallacy." Then the word, "argument." Then the acronym. With each word Siri would give me the first definition, then ask if I wanted the next, then the next etc. To suddenly find myself laughing as I realized the amazing choices being offered to me, of choosing which definition 'I' liked. The importance of the word, "fallacy" ... of mistaking the truth of someone else's belief about a word as truth for me. Then the choice of taking any word and by turning it into an acronym I am virtually creating a new definition of that word. Oh, the fun I have been having in the realizations of the power of words, feelings, experiences and beliefs!!!- Cat Friske

Definitions

Accentuate: To make (something) more prominent or noticeable.

Accept or Acceptance: 1. To receive (something offered) willingly accept, a gift. 2. To give admittance or approval to. 3. To recognize as true: believe. 4. To make a favorable response to. 5. Consent to receive.

Accede: To give consent, approval, or adherence; agree; assent.

Accord: 1. To be in agreement or harmony; agree. To grant; bestow. 2. Consent or concurrence of opinions or wills; agreement. 3. To bring into agreement.

Acknowledge: 1. To recognize the rights, authority, or status of. (Acknowledge yourself as the authority in your own life.) (What you believe, is your reality). 2. To disclose knowledge of or agreement with. 3. To express gratitude or obligation for. 4. To make known the receipt of. (Always acknowledge the good that comes into your life.)

Admit: 1. To allow entry. 2. To give entrance or access. 3. To make acknowledgment. 4. To give right or means of entrance to. 5. To permit to exercise a certain function or privilege.

Agreement - Harmony or accordance in opinion or feeling; a position or result of agreeing.

Look closely... HARMONY in FEELING. We know that feeling is the secret of creation... when we agree with something that we hear or read, and it creates a feeling, we are drawing that thing or experience into our lives.

Anticipation: The action of anticipating something; expectation or prediction.

142

Appreciation: 1. A full understanding of a situation. 2. A feeling or expression of admiration, approval, or gratitude. 3. Clear perception or recognition.

Apprehend or Apprehending: 1. Understand or perceive.2. To become aware of.

Ask: 1. The act or an instance of asking for something. 2. Something asked for. 3. The state of being sought after. 4. To call for. 5. To make a request. 6. To put a question to; inquire of. 7. To try to get by using words; request.

Assent: 1. To agree or concur; subscribe to. 2. To give in; yield; concede. 3. Agreement, as to a statement, proposal, etc; acceptance.

Assume - Assumption: 1. Suppose to be the case, without proof. 2. Take or begin to have (power or responsibility). 3. A thing that is accepted as true or as certain to happen, without proof. 4. The action of taking or beginning to take power or responsibility. 5. The act of laying claim to or taking possession of something.

Attractive: Possessing the ability to draw or pull.

Attraction: 1. The act, process, or power of attracting. 2. The action or power of drawing forth a response. 3. A force acting mutually between particles of matter, tending to draw them together, and resisting their separation. 4. A person or thing that draws, attracts, allures, or entices.

Attention: 1. The act or state of applying the mind to something. 2. A condition of readiness for such attention involving especially a selective narrowing or focusing of consciousness and receptivity.

Authority: 1. Power to influence or command Thought, opinion, or behavior. 2. Convincing force. 3. The right to control, command, or determine. 4. A power or right delegated or given.

Auto-Suggestion: 1. An influencing of one's own attitudes, behavior, or physical condition by mental processes other than conscious Thought. 2. Suggestion arising from oneself, as the repetition of verbal messages as a means of changing behavior. (See Suggestion)

Awareness: 1. Knowledge or perception of a situation or fact. 2. The quality or state of being aware. 3. Knowledge and understanding that something is happening or exists. 4. The state or condition of being aware; having knowledge; consciousness.

Beget: 1. To procreate or generate. 2. To cause; produce as an effect.

Being: 1. The fact of existing; existence (as opposed to nonexistence). 2. Conscious, mortal existence; life. 3. Substance or nature. 4. Something that exists. 5. That which has actuality either materially or in idea. 6. absolute existence in a complete or perfect state, lacking no essential characteristic; essence.

Belief - Believe: 1. An acceptance that a statement is true or that something exists. 2. Trust, faith, or confidence in someone or something. 3. Conviction of the truth of some statement or the reality of some being or phenomenon especially when based on examination of evidence. 4. To accept the word or evidence of. 5. To have a conviction that (a person or thing) is, has been, or will be engaged in a given action or involved in a given situation.

Cause: 1. A person or thing that acts, happens, or exists in such a way that some specific thing happens as a result; the producer of an effect. 2. Something that brings about an effect or a result.

144

Cerebration: The working of the brain; thinking.

Cognition: The action of thinking deeply about something; contemplation.

Clarity: 1. The quality of being clear, in particular. 2. The quality of being easy to see or hear; sharpness of image or sound. 3. The quality of being easily understood.

Command: 1. To direct authoritatively: order. 2. To exercise a dominating influence over. 3. To demand or receive as one's due. 4. To overlook or dominate from or as if from a strategic position. 5. To order or request to be given. 6. To have or exercise direct authority: govern. 7. To deserve and receive.

Commensurate: 1. Corresponding in size, extent, amount, or degree. 2 Equal in measure or extent.

Conceive: 1. Become pregnant with (A desire). 2. Form or devise (a plan or idea) in the mind. 3. To cause to begin: originate. 4. to apprehend by reason or imagination.

Concentration: 1. The action or power of focusing one's attention or mental effort. 2. Exclusive attention to one object; close mental application.

Concept: 1. A plan or intention; a conception. 2. Something conceived in the mind.

Concluding: 1. Bring (something) to an end. 2. Arrive at a judgment or opinion by reasoning.

Concord: 1. Agreement or harmony between people or groups. 2. Agreement between words in gender, number, case, person, or any other grammatical category that affects the forms of the words.

Condition: 1. A premise upon which the fulfillment of an agreement depends. 2. Something essential to the appearance or occurrence of something else. 3. A state of being. 4. A particular mode of being of a person or thing; existing state; situation with respect to circumstances. 5. A circumstance indispensable to some result; prerequisite; that on which something else is contingent.

Connote: 1. Imply or suggest (an idea or feeling) in addition to the literal or primary meaning. 2. To convey in addition to exact explicit meaning. 3. To be associated with or inseparable from as a consequence or concomitant 4. to involve as a condition or accompaniment.

Consciousness: 1. The state of being conscious; awareness of one's own existence, sensations, Thoughts, surroundings, etc. 2. The Thoughts and feelings, collectively, of an individual or of an aggregate of people. 3. Full activity of the mind and senses, as in waking life. 4. Awareness of something for what it is; internal knowledge. 5. The mental activity of which a person is aware as contrasted with unconscious mental processes. 6. The mind or the mental faculties as characterized by Thought, feelings, and volition. 7. The quality or state of being aware especially of something within oneself. 8. The upper level of mental life of which the person is aware as contrasted with unconscious processes.

Consideration: 1. Continuous and careful Thought. 2. A matter weighed or taken into account when formulating an opinion or plan. 3. An opinion obtained by reflection

Contemplation: 1. A: Concentration on spiritual things as a form of private devotion. B: A state of mystical awareness of God's being. 2. An act of considering with attention. 3. The act of regarding steadily.

Contract: 1. A written or spoken agreement that is intended to be enforceable by law. 2. Enter into a formal and legally binding agreement. 3. The written form of such an agreement. 4. To settle or establish by agreement.

Covenant: 1. A usually formal, solemn, and binding agreement. 2. A written agreement or promise usually under seal between two or more parties especially for the performance of some action.

Creation: The action or process of bringing something into existence.

Decree: 1. A formal and authoritative order, especially one having the force of law. 2. To command, ordain, or decide by decree. 3. To command or enjoin by or as if by decree.

Deduction: 1. The deriving of a conclusion by reasoning. 2. A conclusion reached by logical deduction. *(Something to remember: The Subconscious Mind works by deduction. This is why Imagining FROM the end works. It does not work by Induction. What this means is you do not tell it what you want, but what you already have. Then it, the Subconscious Mind, will find the ways and means of bringing it to fruition. Your job is to give it the fulfilled desire, not how you want to make it happen.)*

Deliberate: 1. Carefully weighed or considered; studied; intentional. 3. Characterized by deliberation or cautious consideration; careful or slow in deciding. 4. Done consciously and intentionally.

Deliberation: 1. The act of thinking about or discussing something and deciding carefully.

Demonstration: 1. The act or circumstance of proving or being proved conclusively, as by reasoning or a show of evidence. 2. Something serving as proof or supporting evidence. 3. A description or explanation, as of a process, illustrated by examples, specimens, or the like. 4. An exhibition, as of feeling; display; manifestation. 5. An outward expression or display. 6. An act of showing someone how something is used or done. 7. To manifest or exhibit; show.

Deriving: 1. To take, receive, or obtain especially from a specified source. 2. What was derived from their observations.

Desire: 1. A strong feeling of wanting to have something or wishing for something to happen. 2. Strongly wish for or want (something). 3. To long or hope for: exhibit or feel desire for.

Discerning: Showing insight and understanding.

Dormant: 1. Marked by a suspension of activity: such as A: temporarily devoid of external activity. B. Temporarily in abeyance yet capable of being activated. C. Not actively growing but protected from the environment. 2. Lying asleep or as if asleep; inactive, as in sleep. 3. In a state of rest or inactivity; inoperative; in abeyance. 4. In a state of minimal metabolic activity with cessation of growth, either as a reaction to adverse conditions or as part of an organism's normal annual rhythm.

Educe: To bring out (something, such as something latent)

Effect: 1. A change that is a result or consequence of an action or other cause. 2. Cause (something) to happen; bring about. 3. An outward sign 4. Power to produce results; efficacy; force; validity; influence.

Eliminate: 1. To put an end to or get rid of, especially as being in some way undesirable: remove. 2. To expel (waste) from the living body. 3. To cause to disappear by combining two or more equations. 3. To omit, especially as being unimportant or irrelevant; leave out.

Elicit: 1. Evoke or draw out (a response, answer, or fact) from someone in reaction to one's own actions or questions. 2. Draw forth (something that is latent or potential) into existence.

Look very carefully at the above definitions of elicit. Questions are literally drawing forth something that is latent within us, into existence for us to experience without.

Elude: To escape the understanding, perception, appreciation or grasp of.

Emanation: 1. An abstract but perceptible thing that issues or originates from a source. 2. The action or process of issuing from a source. 3. The origination of the world by a series of hierarchically descending radiations from the Godhead through intermediate stages to matter.

Enchant: 1. To subject to magical influence; bewitch.

Entity: 1. Being, existence; especially: independent, separate, or self-contained existence. 2. Something that has separate and distinct existence and objective or conceptual reality. 3. Essential nature.

Envisage: 1. To have a mental picture of especially in advance of realization. 2. To view or regard in a certain way. 3. Contemplate or conceive of as a possibility or a desirable future event. Synonyms: picture, imagine, conceive, envision.

Equivalent: 1. Equal in value, measure, force, effect, significance, etc. 2. Having the same capacity to combine or react chemically. 3. Something that is equivalent. 4. Like in signification or import. 5. Having the same chemical combining capacity.

Evoke: 1. Bring or recall to the conscious mind. 2. Invoke (a spirit or deity).

Express: 1. Directly, firmly, and explicitly stated. 2. To put (Thought) into words; utter or state. 3. To show, manifest, or reveal. 4. To set forth the opinions, feelings, etc., of (oneself), as in speaking, writing, or painting. 5. To represent by a symbol, character, figure, or formula. 6. Clearly indicated; distinctly stated; definite; explicit; plain.

Fallacy: 1. A mistaken belief, especially one based on unsound argument. 2. A false or mistaken idea. 3. Deceptive appearance 4. A wrong belief: a false or mistaken idea.

Focus: 1. A central point, as of attraction, attention, or activity. 2. The clear and sharply defined condition of an image. 3. The position of a viewed object or the adjustment of an optical device necessary to produce a clear image. 4. Directed attention.

Foreordain: 1. To predestine; predetermine. 2. To ordain or appoint beforehand.

Forgive: 1. Stop feeling angry or resentful toward (someone) for an offense, flaw, or mistake. 2. Cancel (a debt). 3. To cease to feel resentment against (an offender): Pardon; Forgive one's enemies. (To forgive means to let go, to be free of (something) that harms you - David Allen)

Generate: 1. To bring into existence; cause to be; produce. 2. To create by a vital or natural process. 3. To create and distribute vitally and profusely. 4. To reproduce; procreate. 5. To produce by a chemical process. 6. To be the cause of (a situation, action, or state-of-mind) 7. To define or originate something by the application of one or more rules or operations.

Gratitude: 1. The quality of being thankful; readiness to show appreciation for and to return kindness. 2. A feeling of appreciation.

Harmony: Agreement or concord.

Hope: 1. To desire with expectation of obtainment or fulfillment. 2. To expect with confidence.

Heed: To pay attention.

Idea: 1. Any conception existing in the mind as a result of mental understanding, awareness, or activity. 2. A Thought, conception, or notion. 3. An impression. 4. A transcendent entity that is a real pattern of which existing things are imperfect representations. 5. An entity (such as a Thought, concept, sensation, or image) actually or potentially present to consciousness.

Ideation: 1. The capacity for or the act of forming or entertaining ideas. 2. The process of forming ideas or images.

Impart: 1. Make (information) known; communicate. 2. Bestow (a quality). 3. To give, convey, or grant from or as if from a store.

Inducing: 1. To move by persuasion or influence. 2. To call forth or bring about by influence or stimulation. 3. To cause the formation of. 4. To produce by induction. 5. To determine by induction. 6. To lead or move by persuasion or influence, as to some action or state-of-mind. 7. To bring about, produce, or cause.

Infer: 1. To derive by reasoning; conclude or judge from premises or evidence. 2. (of facts, circumstances, statements, etc.) to indicate or involve as a conclusion; lead to. 3. To involve as a normal outcome of Thought. 4. To derive as a conclusion from facts or premises.

Imagination: 1. The faculty of imagining, or of forming mental images or concepts of what is not actually present to the senses; the action or process of forming such images or concepts. 2. The act or power of forming a mental image of something not present to the senses or never before wholly perceived in reality. 3. Creative ability. 4. A creation of the mind. 5. The thinking or active mind. 6. The ability of the mind to be creative or resourceful.

Impression: 1. A characteristic, trait, or feature resulting from some influence. 2. A telling image impressed on the senses or the mind. 3. A communicating of a mold, trait, or character by an external force or influence.

Influence: 1. The capacity to have an effect on the character, development, or behavior of someone or something, or the effect itself. 2. An emanation of spiritual or moral force. 3. The act or power of producing an effect without apparent exertion of force or direct exercise of command. 4. The power or capacity of causing an effect in indirect or intangible ways.

Inquisitive: 1. Given to inquiry, research, or asking questions; eager for knowledge; intellectually curious. 2. Given to examination or investigation.

Insight: 1. An instance of apprehending the true nature of a thing, especially through intuitive understanding. 2. Penetrating mental vision or discernment; faculty of seeing into inner character or underlying truth. 3. An understanding of relationships that sheds light on or helps solve a problem.

Interpreting: 1. To explain or tell the meaning of: present in understandable terms. 2. To conceive in the light of individual belief, judgment, or circumstance.

Introspection: 1. A reflective looking inward. 2. An examination of one's own Thoughts and feelings. 2. Observation or examination of one's own mental and emotional state, mental processes, etc.; the act of looking within oneself.

Intuition: 1. Direct perception of truth, fact, etc., independent of any reasoning process; immediate apprehension. 2. Immediate apprehension or cognition. 3.

The power or faculty of attaining to direct knowledge or cognition without evident rational Thought and inference

Inviting: 1. Offering the promise of an attractive or enjoyable experience. 2. To request politely or formally. 3. To act so as to bring on or render probable. 4. To call forth.

(My questions invited the experiences I asked for, into my life.)

Invoke - 1. Call on (a deity or spirit) in prayer, as a witness, or for inspiration. 2. Call earnestly for.

Knowing: 1. Indicating possession of exclusive inside knowledge or information. 2. affecting, implying, or deliberately revealing shrewd knowledge of secret or private information.

Latent: 1. Existing but not yet developed or manifest; hidden; concealed. 2. Lying dormant or hidden until circumstances are suitable for development or manifestation. 3. Present but not visible, apparent, or actualized; existing as potential. 4. Existing in unconscious or dormant form but potentially able to achieve expression. 5. Present and capable of emerging or developing but not now visible, obvious, active, or symptomatic. 6. Synonyms of Latent: dormant, quiescent, veiled, potential refer to powers or possibilities existing but hidden or not yet actualized. Latent emphasizes the hidden character or the dormancy of what is named: latent qualities.

Law: A statement of fact, deduced from observation, to the effect that a particular natural or scientific phenomenon always occurs if certain conditions are present.

Logic: 1. A science that deals with the principles and criteria of validity of inference and demonstration. 2. Interrelation or sequence of facts or events when seen as inevitable or predictable. 3. Something that forces a decision apart from or in opposition to reason.

Magic: 1. The power of apparently influencing the course of events by using mysterious or supernatural forces. 2. The art of producing a desired effect or result through the use of incantation or various other techniques that presumably assure human control of supernatural agencies or the forces of nature. 3. The effects produced. any extraordinary or mystical influence, charm, power, etc.

(Note: *Words are magic. This is what words do. They perform magic.)*

Manifest: 1. Readily perceived by the eye or the understanding; evident; obvious; apparent; plain. 2. Of or relating to conscious feelings, ideas, and impulses that contain repressed psychic material. 3. To make clear or evident to the eye or the understanding; show plainly. 4. To prove; put beyond doubt or question. 5. Easily understood or recognized by the mind.

Matrix: 1. An environment or material in which something develops; a surrounding medium or structure. 2. Something that constitutes the place or point from which something else originates, takes form, or develops.

Meditation: 1. Continued or extended Thought; reflection; contemplation. 2. To engage in Thought or contemplation; reflect.

Mindset: 1. The established set of attitudes held by someone. 2. An attitude, disposition, or mood. 3. An intention or inclination. 4. A fixed mental attitude or disposition that predetermines a person's responses to and interpretations of situations. 5. A fixed state-of-mind

Mulling: 1. To consider at length: ponder. 2. To study or ruminate. 3. To think about carefully; consider.

Muse: 1. To become absorbed in Thought; especially: to think about something carefully and thoroughly. 2. To think or meditate in silence, as on some subject.

Mystical: 1. Inspiring a sense of spiritual mystery, awe, and fascination. 2. Having a spiritual meaning or reality that is neither apparent to the senses nor obvious to the intelligence. 3. Involving or having the nature of an individual's direct subjective communion with God (Consciousness) or ultimate reality. 4. Mystic; of or relating to supernatural agencies, affairs, occurrences, etc. 5. Spiritually symbolic.

Negative - Negativity: 1. consisting in or characterized by the absence rather than the presence of distinguishing features. 2. (of a person, attitude, or situation) not desirable or optimistic. 3. A word or statement that expresses denial, disagreement, or refusal. 4. The expression of criticism of or pessimism about something. 5. Lacking in constructiveness, helpfulness, optimism, cooperativeness, or the like.

Observe: 1. Notice or perceive (something) and register it as being significant. 2. Fulfill or comply with. 3. To conform one's action or practice to something. 4. To watch carefully especially with attention to details or behavior for the purpose of arriving at a judgment. 5. To come to realize or know especially through consideration of noted facts.

Perceive: 1. To become aware of, know, or identify by means of the senses. 2. To recognize, discern, envision, or understand. 2. To attain awareness or understanding of.

Permission: 1. Authorization granted to do something; formal consent. 2. The act of permitting. 3. Formal consent.

Ponder: To think or consider especially quietly, soberly, and deeply; Meditate.

Positive - Positivity: 1. Consisting in or characterized by the presence or possession of features or qualities rather than their absence. 2. with no possibility of doubt; clear and definite. 3. A good, affirmative, or constructive quality or attribute. 4. The practice of being or tendency to be positive or optimistic in attitude. 5. The presence rather than absence of a certain substance, condition, or feature.

Potential: 1. Having or showing the capacity to become or develop into something in the future. 2. Latent qualities or abilities that may be developed and lead to future success or usefulness.

Principle: 1. A moral rule or belief that helps you know what is right and wrong and that influences your actions. 2. A basic truth or theory: an idea that forms the basis of something. 3. A law or fact of nature that explains how something works or why something happens. 4. A general or basic truth on which other truths or theories can be based. 5. A law or fact of nature which makes possible the working of a machine or device. 6. According to a fixed rule, method, or practice.

Proclaim: 1. Declare something one considers important with due emphasis. 2. Declare officially to be. 3. To give outward indication of. 4. To declare or declare to be solemnly, officially, or formally. 5. To announce or declare in an official or formal manner. (interesting note about the word proclaim ... Manifest is a synonym of Proclaim.)

Program - Programming: 1. A plan of action to accomplish a specified end. 2. A planned, coordinated group of activities, procedures, etc., often for a specific purpose, or a facility offering such a series of activities. 3. The process of instructing or learning by means of an instructional program.

Predestine: To destine, decree, determine, appoint, or settle beforehand.

Proof: 1. Evidence sufficient to establish a thing as true, or to produce belief in its truth. 2. Anything serving as such evidence. 3. The act of testing or making trial of anything; test; trial. 4. The establishment of the truth of anything; demonstration. 5. The effect of evidence in convincing the mind.

Prosperity: 1. The condition of being successful or thriving; especially: economic well-being. 2. The state of being successful usually by making money. 3. A successful, flourishing, or thriving condition, especially in financial respects; good fortune.

Quiescent: 1. Being at rest; quiet; still; inactive or motionless. 2. marked by inactivity or repose: tranquilly at rest.

Rationalize: To ascribe (one's acts, opinions, etc.) to causes that superficially seem reasonable and valid but that actually are unrelated to the true, possibly unconscious and often less creditable or agreeable causes.

React: 1. Respond or behave in a particular way in response to something. 2. To exert a reciprocal or counteracting force or influence. 3. To change in response to a stimulus.

Reaction: 1. An action performed or a feeling experienced in response to a situation or event. 2. A person's ability to respond physically and mentally to external stimuli. 3. Resistance or opposition to a force, influence, or movement. 4. Bodily response to or activity aroused by a stimulus. 5. The force that a body subjected to the action of a force from another body exerts in the opposite direction.

Realize: 1. To bring into concrete existence. 2. To conceive vividly as real: be fully aware of. 3. To bring vividly to the mind. 4. To grasp or understand clearly.

Reasoning: The process of forming conclusions, judgments, or inferences from facts or premises.

Receptive: 1. Having the quality of receiving, taking in, or admitting. 2. Willing or inclined to receive suggestions, offers, etc., with favor. 3. Willing to consider or accept new suggestions and ideas. 4. Able or willing to receive something, especially signals or stimuli.

Recognition: 1. An act of recognizing or the state of being recognized. 2. The identification of something as having been previously seen, heard, known, etc. 3. The perception of something as existing or true; realization. 4. The acknowledgment of something as valid or as entitled to consideration. 5. The expression of this in the form of some token of appreciation.

Reflection: 1. An instance of reflecting. 2. The production of an image by or as if by a mirror. 2. An image given back by a reflecting surface. 3. A Thought, idea, or opinion formed, or a remark made as a result of meditation.

Regard: To look upon or think of with a particular feeling.

Regenerate: 1. To re-create, reconstitute, or make over, especially in a better form or condition. 2. To revive or produce anew; bring into existence again. 3. To renew or restore. 4. To cause to be born again spiritually. 5. To come into existence or be formed again. 6. To produce a regenerative effect.

Related: 1. Associated with the specified item or process, especially causally. 2. Having close harmonic connection.

Request: 1. The act or an instance of asking for something. 2. Something asked for. 3. The condition or fact of being. 4. The state of being sought after.

Rumination: 1. To meditate or muse; ponder. 2. To go over in the mind repeatedly and often casually or slowly. 3. To engage in contemplation.

Reflection: 1. The production of an image by or as if by a mirror. 2. Something produced by reflecting: such as a: an image given back by a reflecting surface b: an effect produced by an influence. 3. A Thought, idea, or opinion formed, or a remark made as a result of meditation. 4. Consideration of some subject matter, idea, or purpose.

Revoke: Put an end to the validity or operation of (a decree, decision, or promise).

Responsive: 1. Responding especially readily and sympathetically to appeals, efforts, influences. 2. Giving response: constituting a response: answering. 3. React appropriately.

Reveal: 1. To make known through divine inspiration. 2. To make (something secret or hidden) publicly or generally known; reveal a secret. 3. To lay open to view; display; exhibit. 4. To make known; disclose; divulge.

Secrecy: 1. The state or condition of being secret, hidden, or concealed. 2. The state of being apart from other people; privacy; seclusion. 3. The habit or practice of keeping secrets or maintaining privacy or concealment. (Silence and Secrecy are synonyms)

Science: 1. The state of knowing: knowledge as distinguished from ignorance or misunderstanding. 2. Knowledge or a system of knowledge covering general truths, or the operation of general laws especially as obtained and tested through scientific method. 3. Knowledge about or study of the natural world based on facts learned through experiments and observation.

See: 1. To perceive with the eyes; look at. 2. To perceive (things) mentally; discern; understand. 3. To construct a mental image of; visualize. 4. To accept or imagine or suppose as acceptable. 5. To be cognizant of; recognize.

Self-fulfilling and or Self-fulfilling Prophecy: 1. Becoming real or true by virtue of having been predicted or expected. 2. Marked by or achieving self-fulfillment. 3. A prophecy that comes true because of the expectation that it will. In effect, it's a self-fulfilling prophecy. Talk of recession is a self-fulfilling prophecy. Fear of failure can become a self-fulfilling prophecy.

Silence: 1. Absence of any sound or noise; stillness. 2. The state or fact of being silent. 3. Concealment; secrecy. 4. Absence of mention.(Silence and Secrecy are synonyms)

Source: 1. Any thing or place from which something comes, arises, or is obtained; origin. 2. A point of origin or procurement: beginning.

Speculation: 1. Assumption of unusual business risk in hopes of obtaining commensurate gain.

(*While this definition of speculation uses business as an example let's consider the word, ASSUMPTION, as Neville Goddard says, "Assumptions Harden Into Fact." It can easily be seen that assumptions of anything are creative, such as assuming that a desire is already fulfilled.*)

Spirit: 1. An animating or vital principle held to give life to physical organisms. 2. The activating or essential principle influencing a person. 3. A special attitude or frame of mind. 3. A special attitude or frame of mind.

Spiritual: 1. Relating to or affecting the human spirit or soul as opposed to material or physical things. 2. Of, relating to, consisting of, or affecting the spirit. 3. Of or relating to supernatural beings or phenomena.

Success: 1. The accomplishment of an aim or purpose. 2. A person or thing that achieves desired aims or attains prosperity. 3. The favorable or prosperous termination of attempts or endeavors; the accomplishment of one's goals. 4. The attainment of wealth, position, honors, or the like.

Suggestion: 1. The act of suggesting. 2. The calling up in the mind of one idea by another by virtue of some association or of some natural connection between the ideas. 3. The process of inducing a Thought, sensation, or action in a receptive person without using persuasion and without giving rise to reflection in the recipient. 4. The process by which a physical or mental state is influenced by a Thought or idea. (See Auto-Suggestion)

Understanding: 1. A mental grasp 2. The power of comprehending; especially: the capacity to apprehend general relations of particulars. 3. Friendly or harmonious relationship. 4. An agreement of opinion or feeling. 5. A mutual agreement not formally entered into but in some degree binding on each side.

Veiled: 1. Covered or concealed by, or as if by, a veil. 2. Not openly or directly expressed; masked; disguised; hidden; obscure. 3. Something that covers, separates, screens, or conceals. 4. To hide the real nature of; mask; disguise.

Visualize: 1. To recall or form mental images or pictures. 2. To make perceptible to the mind or imagination. 3. To see or form a mental image of.

Wonder: 1. To think or speculate curiously. 2. To be filled with admiration, amazement, or awe; marvel. 3. Desire or be curious to know something.

Wisdom: 1. The quality of having experience, knowledge, and good judgment; the quality of being wise. 2. The soundness of an action or decision with regard to the application of experience, knowledge, and good judgment. 3. The body of knowledge and principles that develops within a specified society or period.

Metaphysical / Law of Attraction Books

David Allen - The Power of I AM (2014), The Power of I AM - Volume 2 (2015) , The Power of I AM - Volume 3 (2017)

David Allen - The Creative Power of Thought, Man's Greatest Discovery (2017)

David Allen - The Secrets, Mysteries & Powers of The Subconscious Mind (2017)

David Allen - The Money Bible - The Spiritual Secrets of Attracting Prosperity and Abundance (2017)

David Allen - Your Faith Is Your Fortune, Your Unlimited Power (2018)

The Neville Goddard Collection (All 10 of his books plus 2 Lecture series) (2016)

Neville Goddard - Assumptions Harden Into Facts: The Book (2016)

Neville Goddard - Imagination: The Redemptive Power in Man (2016)

Neville Goddard - The World is At Your Command - The Very Best of Neville Goddard (2017)

Neville Goddard - Imagining Creates Reality - 365 Mystical Daily Quotes (2017)

Neville Goddard's Interpretation of Scripture (2018)

The Definitive Christian D. Larson Collection (6 Volumes, 30 books) (2014)

David Allen - ASKffirmations (2018)

Recommended Reading

Abraham-Hicks - Ask and It is Given

Abraham-Hicks - The Amazing Power Of Deliberate Intent

Ernest Holmes - Creative Mind

Florence Scovel Shinn - The Power of the Spoken Word

Jack Canfield - The Power of Focus

James Allen - As a Man Thinketh

Joe Dispenza - Evolve Your Brain

Joe Vitale - The Attractor Factor

Joel S. Goldsmith - Consciousness Unfolding

Joel S. Goldsmith - Invisible Supply

Joseph Murphy - The Power of Your Subconscious Mind

Louise Hay - You Can Heal Your Life

Noah St. John - The Great Little Book of Afformations

Norman Vincent Peale - The Power Of Positive Thinking

Prentice Mulford - Your Forces and How To Use Them

Ralph Waldo Trine - In Tune With The Infinite

Rhonda Byrne - The Secret

Visit us at **NevilleGoddardBooks.com** for 1000's of Free Downloadable eBooks on Metaphysics, Law of Attraction, Oriental Philosophy, Ancient Secrets, plus much more.

Also Check out our friends at **TheIAMLibrary.com** for more eBooks and Audio. You'll be glad you did.

CPSIA information can be obtained
at www.ICGtesting.com
Printed in the USA
LVHW03s0759170918
590361LV00001B/42/P